WINNING MONEY FOR COLLEGE

WINNING MONEY FOR COLLEGE

The High School Student's Guide to Scholarship Contests

Alan Deutschman

Peterson's Guides
Princeton, New Jersey

Library of Congress Cataloging in Publication Data

Deutschman, Alan.
  Winning money for college.

  Includes index.
  1. Scholarships—United States—Handbooks, manuals, etc. I. Title.
LB2338.D48 1984   378'.34'0973   83-22151
ISBN 0-87866-261-8

Printed in the United States of America

10 9 8 7 6 5 4 3 2 1

For other Peterson's publications of interest, please see the annotated book list at the back of this volume.

Essay on page 49 © 1983 by Charles Cohen. Reprinted by permission.

Essay on page 81 © 1983 by Guideposts Associates, Inc., Carmel, NY 10512. All rights reserved. Reprinted by permission.

To my parents

ACKNOWLEDGMENTS

I would like to express my appreciation to all those individuals who helped in the research and preparation of this book. I am grateful to numerous program directors and officials for their assistance in two vital capacities: providing detailed information and carefully reviewing the manuscript for accuracy. High school students also played a major role in supplying information, and I am indebted to the many students who offered comments and insights either in personal conversations or by completing questionnaire forms. A special note of gratitude must also be given to the students and contest officials who consented to have winning entries (essays, speeches, etc.) appear or be excerpted in this volume. In addition, I want to acknowledge the kind permission of the following organizations to reprint material in this book: the American Association of Teachers of German, for test questions from the 1983 National German Examination for High School Students; the American Association of Teachers of Italian, for test questions from the 1983 AATI National Contest; the American Classical League and the National Junior Classical League, for test questions from the 1983 National Latin Exam; and the Quill and Scroll Society, for test questions from the 1983 Quill and Scroll Current Events Quiz.

Most important, I am deeply grateful to my parents, Hal and Elaine, and my brother, Robert, for their encouragement and advice during this entire project, and for their love and support always.

CONTENTS

Contents

How to Win Scholarship Money

The Unknown Source of College Money

There probably isn't a college-bound student in the nation who is unaware of the difficulty of financing an education today. The cost of one year at several well-known private universities has skyrocketed to over $15,000 and is rising steadily, while tuition costs at public institutions are increasing as well. Applying for financial aid is the answer for those who clearly can demonstrate need. What about students who don't quite qualify but who know paying college bills will still be very hard on their families? What about students whose preliminary analysis shows they won't get as much aid as their family feels they need? What about students who have demonstrated outstanding talent and would like to be rewarded for it? For all students of accomplishment who are seeking additional sources of college money, there is a large and too often overlooked reservoir of funds to tap: privately sponsored merit scholarships. A merit scholarship is one that is based on specified performance or accomplishments in some field, rather than on financial need. Most colleges today offer their own merit scholarships, but this book covers the national competitions that are open to anyone with the skills and background to enter and that allow the winners to attend a college of their own choosing.

Scholarships: Myths and Misconceptions

The scholarship game is highly misunderstood by many high school students. It is common for teenagers to think that scholarships are rare, elusive awards won only by valedictorians, geniuses, and "whiz kids." High school guidance counselors, overburdened with paperwork and complaints, often lack the time to fully investigate scholarship opportunities and inform students about them. The myths and misconceptions persist, while the truth about scholarships remains hidden, the glittering prizes and benefits unknown to many teenagers.

These are the facts: with proper advice and strategies, private scholarships are within the grasp of high school students who possess

1

talent and ability in almost any given field. Academic achievement is not the only basis for these scholarships. Many of the best opportunities are in such areas as writing, public speaking, leadership, science, community service, music and the arts, foreign languages, and vocational-technical skills. For women, minority students, and members of national clubs and student organizations (such as 4-H and National Honor Society), the scholarship opportunities are even broader.

There are three basic types of merit-based scholarship competitions. First, there are programs that offer scholarships and awards primarily on the basis of specific performance in some area—through competitive judging of student writing, speeches, projects, artwork, performance, or special tests. Second, there are programs that evaluate a student's past achievements in areas that may include academics, leadership, or involvement in school and community. And third, there are programs that base awards on both past and present achievement, by evaluating past academic records and outside activities as well as performance in a current competition.

The Benefits of Competing

Many programs offer substantial scholarships to winners on the local or county level. For participants who advance to state or national competition, scholarships can reach into the stratosphere of thousands of dollars. For example, first-place national winners in major competitions can be awarded $25,000 (America's Junior Miss), $24,000 (Elks National Foundation), $17,000 (American Legion Oratory), $14,000 (Voice of Democracy), $12,000 (Westinghouse Science Talent Search), or $11,500 (Century III Leaders).

The following list shows the dozen "richest" scholarship programs included in this book and the total amount of money they awarded to high school students in 1983.

1. National Merit Scholarship Program . $25,000,000 (approx.)
2. America's Junior Miss   2,500,000
3. Arts Recognition and Talent Search . .   2,100,000
4. Elks National Foundation Most Valuable Student Scholarship Contest   2,039,000
5. National Achievement Scholarship Program for Outstanding Negro Students . . . .   2,000,000 (approx.)
6. Voice of Democracy Scholarship Program . . . .   607,500+

7. National Honor Society Scholarship
   Program   250,000
8. Century III Leaders Program   218,000
9. U.S. Senate Youth Program   208,000
10. Presidential Scholars Program   141,000
11. Westinghouse Science Talent Search .   89,500
12. American Legion Oratorical Contest .   65,000

In addition to gaining a substantial amount of scholarships or cash for college, contest winners often receive many other benefits, ranging from trophies, plaques, and publicity in local and school newspapers to free dinners to study trips to Europe and publication or performance of their works. Contest winners may also be invited to attend all-expense-paid trips to national contests and conventions. At some of these scholarship junkets, national finalists have an opportunity to meet with top-ranking leaders in American government, sometimes even at the White House. (President Reagan has met with winners from the Presidential Scholars, Senate Youth Program, Junior Miss Program, Science Talent Search, Voice of Democracy, and other programs.)

Success in merit-based scholarship contests can play the dual role of helping to *pay* for college and helping the student *get in* to highly selective colleges. Winning an award in a national competitive program is an impressive distinction, demonstrating the student's achievement beyond the confines of the classroom and the school. Even without winning a scholarship, being recognized as a finalist or semifinalist or being given honorable mention can be a valuable credential for college admissions. This is especially true for some of the larger, more prestigious national competitions, such as National Merit and the Westinghouse Science Talent Search.

Motivation—Information—The "Competitive Edge"

The scholarship-seeker needs three things in the quest for college money. First, he or she must have *motivation and drive*—an ability to work with concentrated effort to achieve goals. If you have the motivation, this book can provide you with the other requirements: *information* and the *"competitive edge."* To make you a well-informed scholarship candidate, it presents over fifty of the most outstanding competitions for high school students that offer thousands of awards, with in-depth descriptions of rules and procedures. To give you a competitive edge, effective strategies and helpful hints from scholarship winners and contest officials are included, as well as excerpts from winning speeches and essays and sample test questions from special exams used in some contests.

The Scholarship Game: A Strategic Approach

Before you start off on your odyssey for scholarships and recognition, keep in mind these general insights, strategies, and observations about the scholarship game:

- *Start early.* It is highly advisable to start entering contests early in your high school career. There are even a number of programs that include separate competitions for grades 7–9. In many of the largest scholarship competitions, students who have not won a top prize can enter each year that they are eligible. For experience alone, it is worthwhile to get involved as a freshman or sophomore—and you may become a winner.

- *Begin preparing in advance.* To achieve success in national scholarship contests, it is highly advantageous to begin your preparation with time to spare before the deadlines start creeping up. In such areas as writing and the arts, participants may be required to submit large portfolios of work. Several programs in math and science involve complex, time-consuming projects. Students hoping to win honors in public speaking contests usually benefit from repeated practice. Early preparation is a definite mark of a competitive entrant.

- *The Minuteman approach.* Be ready for whatever opportunities may become available. If you are a senior, a good idea is to keep a file of materials that are often required. By holding on to copies of papers and documents, you can quickly duplicate them and send them off as part of scholarship applications without wasting valuable time. Keep on file copies of at least three recommendations (from your principal or vice-principal, guidance counselor, and one or more teachers) concerning your academic and nonacademic achievements as well as your personal qualities. Keep copies of any general college application essays you have written that can be recycled for scholarship applications. If you have a number of impressive achievements in a certain area (debate victories, athletic awards, published newspaper articles, etc.), list and describe them in a special one-page write-up that can be added to scholarship forms. If you are interested in entering writing competitions, keep on hand neat, typewritten copies of your best work. Program deadlines do not always fall at convenient moments. Time *is* money—scholarship money.

4

- *Make friends with your guidance counselor.* Talk with your counselor at the beginning of the school year, and enlist the counselor's assistance in your efforts to enter and win competitions. Ask your counselor to give you a copy of all information that the school receives about scholarship opportunities in fields that interest you.

- *The "Spillover Effect."* Entering scholarship competitions isn't as much work as it may first appear to be. Students can make their intellectual and creative efforts work overtime for them. You may find that several contests in one field—such as science, public speaking, the arts, or writing—will have similar requirements, and work that was prepared for one contest can be adapted for use in several others.

- *The "Success leads to success" syndrome.* There is a definite cumulative effect in winning competitive awards. Success in performance-oriented competitions forms an impressive background of past achievements when applying for the next competition.

- *Use original material only.* Plagiarism is the fastest way to be eliminated from a program. Be certain to submit your own work only or to give appropriate credit to material taken from other sources.

- *Read all contest materials carefully.* Although this seems obvious, numerous contest officials have pointed out that many students do not pay attention to the rules. Also, make sure to obtain a copy of the most recent brochure to get firsthand information about deadlines, correct entry procedures, and scholarship criteria. It is not advisable to take someone else's word about contest rules, even that of a well-meaning friend or school adviser.

ABOUT THE CONTESTS IN THIS BOOK

This book covers more than 50 programs sponsored by private organizations that provide millions of dollars in scholarship and cash awards to high school students solely on the basis of talent, ability, and achievement. The following specific criteria were imposed in selecting the final group.

- Talent, achievement, and competitive performance are the major bases for selecting winners. (Athletic awards are not included.) Many contests are based primarily on a student's performance in a specified activity, that is, entrants have to do something special for the contest. In others, entrants submit an application describing their previous academic and nonacademic accomplishments.

- All awards have some monetary value.

- The award may be used at the college or university of the winner's choice, with a wide range of institutions to choose from.

- Students who fulfill the basic eligibility requirements can enter the program "under their own steam," i.e., they do not have to wait to be nominated or selected by someone else in order to initiate the application process. The Appendix includes two exceptional programs—the American Academy of Achievement and the Presidential Scholars Program—that choose winners from other contests only; students may not enter these programs by direct application.

- The program is available to contestants on a national basis (although a few are not available in every state or locality).

Who May Enter the Contests

In general, and unless otherwise specified, programs are open to full-time students attending public, private, or parochial secondary schools in the United States (including the 50 states and the District of

Columbia) who are planning to attend an accredited U.S. two- or four-year college or university. If a program is also open to residents of Puerto Rico or the Trust Territories, to American students abroad, or to students in other countries, it is so stated in the capsule summary that precedes each description.

Some programs have minimal restrictions or eligibility requirements; these usually center on grade in school, minimum or maximum age, U.S. citizenship, or career interests in a particular field, such as engineering, public affairs, or journalism. However, a few programs limit eligibility to certain large groups, such as women, minority students, members of specific religious faiths, or members of student or national organizations. *Applicants should pay careful attention to these restrictions and apply only to those programs for which they qualify.*

How the Awards May Be Used

The majority of programs require that applicants plan to attend a two- or four-year college. If the program states that applicants must plan to obtain a bachelor's degree, then a four-year institution is meant. If college attendance is not required, or if the award is for a postsecondary vocational or technical institute or for independent study, this is stated in the capsule summary. The assumption in most contests—indeed the requirement—is that the winners will spend their prize money for further study, and in most cases the money goes directly to the college of each student's choice. However, there are a number of contests that award cash prizes with no requirements and no strings attached. A distinction is made in this book between the more common "scholarship"—money to be used at a college—and "cash prize" or "cash award"—which may be used in any way.

Notes on Reading the Descriptions

All information concerning the rules and requirements of contests included in this book was screened for accuracy by the officials who administer the programs. All dates and statistics refer to the 1983 contests, unless otherwise specified. However, changes in the way programs are conducted may occur on a year-to-year basis. Also, the information printed here is naturally a summary of the complete, official contest rules distributed to high schools and students by the sponsoring organizations. Therefore, it is essential to contact the information sources included at the end of each entry to receive current and precise information and, in some cases, application forms and materials.

Format of the Descriptions

The description of each contest generally follows this format:

- Capsule Summary: a concise listing of the most important information about the contest, including primary focus, eligibility, entry requirements, awards, deadlines, and program sponsors.

- Overview of the Program

- Rules and Procedures

- Helpful Hints

- Samples or Excerpts of Winning Entries or Sample Test Questions

- Program Deadlines

- For More Information/Application Forms: people to see and addresses to write to for information, application forms, and contest rules.

Explanation of Terms Used in the Capsule Summaries

ACH	College Board Achievement Tests
ACT	American College Testing Exam
advanced level	advanced (versus preliminary) level of competition
application	application form
DoD schools	Department of Defense Dependents Schools abroad
focus	interest area or achievement area on which awards are based (public speaking, writing, etc.)
permanent resident	foreign national with permanent residency status in the United States
PR	Puerto Rico
PSAT	Preliminary Scholastic Aptitude Test
recommendation(s)	personal references from teachers, counselors, etc.
SAT	Scholastic Aptitude Test
scholarship	award applied to education costs
sponsor/administrator	sponsor is the organization funding the program; administrator is the organization conducting the program (only one organization is listed if it serves in both capacities)
transcript	official school record

Aid Association for Lutherans Scholarship Programs

Focus: General, nursing, vocational/technical

Who May Enter: High school seniors who are AAL members; the Vocational/Technical School program also open to AAL members who are high school grads (or hold an equivalency diploma)

Entry Requirements: All-College and Competitive Nursing: SAT/ ACT, class rank. *Advanced level:* application, essay, recommendations, transcript
Vocational/Technical: application, recommendations, transcript, work experience

Awards: All-College: (200 +) $500–$1750 renewable scholarships, (200) $500 nonrenewable scholarships
Competitive Nursing: (25 +) $500–$1750 renewable scholarships
Vocational/Technical: (50) $250 or $500 renewable scholarships

Deadline: November 30

Sponsor/Administrator: Aid Association for Lutherans

The Aid Association for Lutherans (AAL) offers a variety of scholarship programs for students in 12th grade who are AAL members. The All-College Scholarship Program provides hundreds of scholarship grants to students planning to enroll in a bachelor's degree program at an accredited college or university. At least 200 of these scholarships are annually renewable grants, in amounts ranging from $500 to $1750 per year. An additional 200 nonrenewable scholarships of $500 each are awarded through the program annually.

The Competitive Nursing Scholarship Program provides scholarship aid for students planning to enroll in a registered nursing (RN) education program accredited by the National League for Nursing. Licensed Practical Nursing (LPN) studies are not covered by this program. At least 25 renewable scholarships are made available each year through the Competitive Nursing program, in amounts ranging from $500 to $1750.

The Aid Association for Lutherans Vocational/Technical School Scholarship Program offers grants for students who plan to pursue a vocational diploma or associate degree at an accredited vocational/technical institute or two-year college. Students may be enrolled on either a full-time or a half-time basis, and they must take courses that relate directly to their stated career objectives. This program is not for students working toward a bachelor's degree or enrolled in avocational ("hobby") courses.

As part of the Vocational/Technical School Program, AAL awards up to 25 renewable scholarships per year to graduating high school seniors. Up to an additional 25 renewable awards are also made available to AAL members who are high school graduates or have a high school equivalency diploma. Students in full-time vo/tech programs receive scholarships of $500 per year until the degree/diploma is received, up to a maximum of two years of full-time studies. Awards for half-time students are $250 per year, renewable until the degree/diploma is received, up to a maximum of four half-time years of study.

Rules and Procedures

All-College and Competitive Nursing Scholarship Programs
Graduating high school seniors who hold an Aid Association for Lutherans certificate of membership and insurance are eligible to participate in the programs. In both competitions, semifinalists are chosen based on their class rank and their test scores on the SAT or the ACT. When taking these tests, students must indicate that they wish to release their test scores to the scholarship program code (0433 for All-College or 0609 for Competitive Nursing). Those selected as semifinalists are contacted by the AAL and asked to submit additional materials, including recommendations; the high school transcript; information on extracurricular activities, leadership qualities, and

church and community experiences; and personal statements by the student. The final winners are selected by independent committees of admissions directors from the fields of higher education and nursing education. Financial need is not a factor in the selection of scholarship winners. Once the winners have been chosen, however, financial information supplied by the parents and the college's estimated costs help determine the amount of the award.

Vocational/Technical School Program

Applicants must hold an Aid Association for Lutherans certificate of membership and insurance and be a graduating high school senior. High school graduates or those with a General Equivalency Diploma (GED) who are enrolled or plan to enroll in an accredited vocational/technical study program are also eligible for the scholarships.

An independent committee of vocational educators chooses the award recipients based on several factors. Recommendations from school advisers and references from employers or other professional people are required. The applicant's academic record and involvement in church and community are reviewed. Another important selection criterion is how well the scholarship candidate defines his or her career objectives. Applicants must also provide information about previous work experience. Financial need is not considered in the selection of scholarship winners.

Program Deadlines

Initial application forms must be submitted by November 30. Students applying for the All-College or Competitive Nursing program may take the SAT or ACT in November or December of their senior year (if more than one set of scores is reported to the AAL scholarship competition, the scores from the most recent test will be used). Applicants to these programs are notified of their status in February, at which time semifinalists are sent additional materials to be completed and returned. Applicants to the Vocational/Technical School program must submit their additional application materials by February 1. Scholarship winners for all three programs are announced in May.

For More Information/Application Forms

Write to: Aid Association for Lutherans
            Member and Family Benefits
            4321 North Ballard Road
            Appleton, Wisconsin 54919

American Association for Gifted Children—Mary Jane and Jerome A. Straka Scholarship Fund

Focus:	Science, math, or economics
Who May Enter:	Students in 12th grade
Entry Requirements:	Application, essay, recommendations, transcript
Awards:	Renewable scholarships (number and amounts vary)
Deadline:	May 31
Sponsor/Administrator:	American Association for Gifted Children

The American Association for Gifted Children (AAGC) is a nonprofit organization devoted to recognizing, benefiting, and stimulating the creative talents of gifted children. The Mary Jane and Jerome A. Straka Scholarship Fund, administered by AAGC, offers grants to promising high school seniors interested in one of the fields of the physical or biological sciences, mathematics, or economics. The grants provide students with annual college scholarships, renewable for up to four years with continued academic excellence. Scholarship winners must reapply each year to renew their awards. The number and value of the awards vary from year to year, depending on the availability of funds.

Rules and Procedures

Only students in the 12th grade are eligible to apply for a scholarship. As part of the application procedure, each scholarship candidate must write a statement on the topic "My View of the Future and How I Might

Contribute to It." Students should demonstrate on the application form a history of curricular and/or extracurricular activities relating in some way to science, mathematics, or economics. The AAGC describes other criteria they consider in selecting scholarship recipients: "The applicant should be of strong character and have positive values. There should be evidence of the applicant's concern for humanity and for the well-being of individuals. There must be evidence of the applicant's intent to earn funds to be used toward the cost of his or her education."

In addition to the application, the Association must receive one recommendation from the student's principal, guidance counselor, or other school personnel, together with one recommendation from another adult. The recommendations should refer to the selection criteria cited above and to other achievements of the applicant, both in and out of school. An official high school record must also be submitted.

The American Association for Gifted Children advises that it is highly desirable for applicants to obtain a recommendation from an AAGC member.

Program Deadlines
All application materials must be submitted by May 31.

For More Information/Application Forms
Write to: American Association for Gifted Children
            15 Gramercy Park
            New York, New York 10003

American Association of Teachers of German Awards Program

Focus:	Foreign language
Who May Enter:	High school students in 2nd-4th yr of German language study; U.S. citizens only. Must be at least 16 years old as of 6/30 to qualify for study trip.
Entry Requirements:	Exam. *Advanced level:* application, interview
Awards:	National: up to 90 study trips to W. Germany Local: cash awards of $100 or less (number varies)
Deadline:	Late November
Sponsor/Administrator:	American Association of Teachers of German/American College Testing Program

The American Association of Teachers of German (AATG) sponsors an awards program for high school students across the nation; the 1983 program had over 16,000 participants. Students scoring at the 90th percentile or above on a standardized German language exam are eligible to win an all-expense-paid, 4-week summer study trip to West Germany. The trip takes students to places of historical and cultural interest, including such well-known cities as Berlin and Nuremberg. During their visit the American students live with German families and attend classes in German language and culture. The number of students who are invited to take the study trips each year varies; for example, there were 69 winners in 1983 and 88 in 1981.

The travel-study program, which is sponsored by the AATG in conjunction with the Federal Republic of Germany's Pedagogical

Exchange Service (PAD), offers qualified students a unique and valuable experience. "The trip to Germany was one of the greatest experiences of my life," comments Rob Andrews of Cherry Hill, New Jersey, who won an AATG/PAD Travel-Study Award in his sophomore year. "It benefits me even now as I look back. I couldn't have had a better time if I had paid for my own trip."

In addition to the travel-study program for top scorers, many local AATG chapters sponsor awards programs through which students receive small cash prizes that may be applied to college costs, together with books, pins, and certificates of merit.

Rules and Procedures

High school students in the second, third, or fourth year of German language study may participate in the awards program. Different examinations are administered at each level. Students are eligible to take the test on the level at which they are currently studying; taking the test below one's level of study, or taking more than one test, will result in exclusion from the awards program. A student's level of study is determined by the credits recorded on his or her high school transcript; previous study in elementary or junior high school is not taken into consideration.

German language teachers must submit an order form to obtain copies of the AATG examinations. There is a registration fee of $3 per student. The tests may be taken by students either at their local high school or at an AATG Chapter Test Center. These centers have been established by AATG chairpersons in sixty regions throughout the nation, and teachers who request that their students be tested at the centers are informed of where and when the testing will occur.

The tests utilize computerized answer sheets and are evaluated by the American College Testing Program (ACT) of Iowa City, Iowa. ACT sends the scores and percentile rankings of students to the authorized test administrator at the high school (or to the student's German teacher, if the exam was taken at a Chapter Test Center). This high school faculty member will also be sent AATG/PAD Travel-Study Award application forms for any students scoring at or above the 90th percentile. AATG forwards the names of up to 50 of the highest-scoring students at each level in each chapter to the local Chapter Awards Committee, which recognizes these students with awards as it sees fit.

Students scoring at or above the 90th percentile must complete the application materials and be interviewed (in German) in order to be considered for an AATG/PAD Travel-Study Award. Not all high-scoring students are eligible to receive the award, however. The German authorities have decreed that recipients must be at least 16 years old as of June 30; must have U.S. citizenship; must not live in a household where German is spoken as the primary language; and must not have lived or traveled for more than a total of 8 weeks in German-speaking countries since reaching the age of 6.

Helpful Hints

The examinations are composed of 100 multiple-choice questions and are given in two sections over the course of an hour. Section 1 (20 minutes) contains 40 questions testing listening comprehension. Section 2 (40 minutes) presents a total of 60 questions in three groups, covering grammar and structure; "situational questions" (which test both reading and conversational skill); and reading comprehension of short passages (each approximately 200 words in length).

Dr. Robert A. Govier, Executive Director of the American Association of Teachers of German, states that the AATG avoids using textbook materials or word lists associated with a particular curriculum as a guide in preparing the annual examinations. He points out that the tests are designed so that students will not have an advantage or disadvantage over other students based on the particular textbooks or study techniques (e.g., the aural-oral teaching method) used at their school.

Students and teachers are encouraged to order the examinations from the previous year in order to become familiar with the testing format. (These examinations are available from the AATG for a nominal fee.) The following remark appeared in a recent AATG analysis of test results: "Using the test as a cramming device will not be promising, but using it for practice and as a diagnostic tool can be of great value."

Rob Andrews advises students to prepare for the test by studying grammar, reading, and word comprehension; he also suggests that students try to maintain a clear, accurate German accent throughout the interview, which counts as a primary factor in the selection of Travel-Study Award winners from the group of leading scorers.

Sample Test Questions

The following are sample questions taken from the 1983 National German Examination for High School Students, Level 4, prepared for the American Association of Teachers of German Awards Program:

Directions: In each of the following questions, a certain situation is suggested. From the four choices given for each question, select the remark that is most likely to be made in the suggested situation.

Als Baumanns mit ihren Kindern am Hafen ankommen, sehen sie enttäuscht, daß der Dampfer, mit dem sie ihren Tagesausflug beginnen wollten, eben abgefahren ist. Frau Baumann regt sich darüber nicht auf und sagt zu ihrem Mann:
A. Ich werde bei solchen Fahrten immer seekrank.
B. Es wird wohl bald der nächste kommen.
C. So eine Fahrt interessiert die Kinder bestimmt nicht.
D. Zum Glück haben die auf uns gewartet.

Familie Bauer ist seit Wochen in der Stadt auf Wohnungssuche. Ihre Bekannten raten ihnen:
A. Versucht es doch mal in der Vorstadt!
B. Kauft euch doch ein neues Auto!
C. Besucht eine größere Universität!
D. Geht mal ins Krankenhaus!

An einem Wochenende im Juli machen Fritz und Heinz eine Wanderung im Gebirge. Es ist bewölkt und sieht nach Regen und Gewitter aus. Heinz meint besorgt:
A. Kannst du nachsehen, wer geklingelt hat?
B. Sollen wir die Feuerwehr anrufen?
C. Könntest du bitte das Fenster schließen?
D. Sollten wir nicht lieber umkehren?

Directions: Each of the sentences in this part has a blank space indicating that a word or phrase has been omitted. From the four choices given for each sentence, select the one that fits grammatically when inserted in the sentence.

Wo kann ich hier . . . Zeitungen bekommen?
A. deutsch
B. deutsche
C. deutscher
D. deutschen

Der Zug kam . . . an, als wir gedacht hatten.
A. ehe
B. bald

C. am ehesten
D. eher

Das ist ja . . . Geschichte!
A. höchst interessant
B. hochinteressant
C. eine höchst interessante
D. einer hochinteressanten

Program Deadlines

German language teachers should submit order forms for the tests by the third week in November.

For More Information

Contact your German language teacher, or write to:

AATG Test Director
523 Building, Suite 201
Route 38
Cherry Hill, New Jersey 08034

American Association of Teachers of Italian National Contest

Focus:	Foreign language
Who May Enter:	Students in 9th-12th grades with 1–4 yrs Italian language study
Entry Requirement:	Exam
Awards:	National: study trip to Italy; (4) $150 and (4) $75 cash awards Local: cash awards (number and amounts vary)
Deadline:	March
Sponsor/Administrator:	American Association of Teachers of Italian

The Long Island chapter of the American Association of Teachers of Italian (AATI) sponsors an annual nationwide contest to stimulate and encourage the study of Italian language and culture. The leading advanced-level contestant wins a six-week summer study trip to Italy.

In addition to the grand prize, cash prizes of $150 for first place and $75 for second place are awarded to contest winners at each of four levels of competition. Many other students receive honorable mention in the contest. Additional prizes are awarded by many of the thirteen other local chapters of the association, with cash amounts and numbers varying from year to year.

Rules and Procedures

Any student in the ninth through the twelfth grade who is currently taking first-, second-, third-, or fourth-year courses in Italian is eligible to participate. The competition centers on a 1-hour written examination of Italian language and culture, which is administered by the chairman of the language department in each high school. The contest is conducted on four separate levels, corresponding to the number of years students have studied Italian. Native Italian students may participate only on Level III and Level IV (third- and fourth-year contests), and native speakers are given more challenging versions of the regular examinations.

The examinations contain sections testing listening comprehension (items are read aloud by a teacher), reading comprehension, vocabulary and grammar, and knowledge of Italian culture. All exams except Level I also test writing skills.

The tests are scored by teachers at the high schools. After grading, each school can send only its best entry at each level to the National Contest Committee to continue in the competition. In order to ensure an objective and fair evaluation of examinations submitted by teachers for competition, the Committee reexamines all tests before the national award winners are determined.

Helpful Hints

Students should sharpen their Italian grammar skills, practice writing in Italian, and read books about Italian culture to prepare for the exam. Advanced students should note that the Level IV exam requires students to choose one of several topics on which to write a composition in Italian of at least 125 words. Lisa Marinelli of Staten Island, New York, the 1982 national grand prize winner, wrote a fictional story based on the topic "A Big Surprise" for her composition. She advises Level IV contestants to become accustomed to writing compositions on topics that require "a lot of imagination, such as 'It's raining outside. I'm all alone in a big house. I hear noises in the kitchen. . . .' " This was another of the possible composition themes on her test.

One factor in the competition that is not mentioned in the literature distributed by AATI is that contest officials may place a call to finalists and conduct a personal interview over the telephone. Participants should be aware of this possibility, which has often come as a complete surprise to finalists in past contests.

Sample Test Questions

The following are sample test questions from the 1983 AATI National Contest:

LEVEL II: Write a well-written paragraph in ITALIAN of ten grammatically correct sentences based on the following subtopics:

1. This morning you left your house at 7:30.
2. At the corner of your street, you met your friend.
3. His name is . . . and he is fifteen years old.
4. Together you went to school.
5. You arrived twenty-five minutes before the first lesson.
6. When the bell rang, all students entered the school.
7. The day passed very quickly.
8. You learned a lot as always.
9. There is a lot of homework today.
10. Tomorrow will be another school day.

LEVEL III: In the space provided on your answer sheet, develop a unified composition of ten grammatically correct sentences in ITALIAN based on the following:

You are visiting Italy and keeping a diary. Write one day's entry (including the date):

1. Your trip is almost over.
2. You have seen most of southern Italy.
3. Tomorrow you will meet some of your friends in Bari.
4. They will show you the city and its people.
5. Then you will go to Naples where you have other friends.
6. You have bought gifts for your friends.
7. You have been studying Italian for three years.
8. You should be able to talk with them.
9. It's been a long day and you must get up early tomorrow to catch the train.
10. You are falling asleep.

LEVEL IV: Using any ONE of the following topics, write a composition in ITALIAN of at least 125 words. Please adhere to the topic.

1. Uno Studente Italiano Con Il Quale Siete in Corrispondenza, Vi Ha Chiesto Informazioni Sulla Vita Del Popolo Americano. Rispondete in Merito!

2. Se Vincessi La Lotteria . . . !
3. Le Mie Aspirazioni Nella Vita.

Program Deadlines

The language examination is held in April. School officials must order copies of the exams by mid-March. Contest winners are announced in May.

For More Information

See the head of the language department of your high school, or write to:

> Professor Giuseppe Battista
> Chairman, AATI National High School Contest
> Suffolk Community College
> Selden, NY 11784

American Classical League/ National Junior Classical League—National Latin Exam

Focus:	Foreign language
Who May Enter:	Students in 9th-12th grades with 1–4 years of Latin study. Also open to students overseas.
Entry Requirements:	Exam. *Advanced level:* application, essay, recommendations
Awards:	(2) $1000 scholarships; gold and silver medals
Deadline:	Early January
Sponsor/Administrator:	American Classical League, National Junior Classical League

More than 35,000 Latin students throughout the world took the National Latin Exam in 1983. Jointly sponsored by the American Classical League (ACL) and the National Junior Classical League (NJCL), this examination gives high school Latin students an opportunity to gain national recognition and scholarship awards. The exam committee remarks in its annual report: "The philosophy of the National Latin Exam is predicated on providing every Latin student with the opportunity to experience a sense of personal accomplishment and success in his study of the Latin language and culture. This opportunity exists for each individual student since, in the National Latin Exam, he is not competing with his fellow students on a comparative basis but is evaluated solely on his own performance on the exam."

Gold and silver medals and merit certificates are awarded to students earning high scores on the examination. In 1983 almost half of the students taking the exam received these awards. The highest scorers compete for two $1000 scholarships (awarded for the first time in 1984).

Rules and Procedures

All high school students enrolled in Latin courses (up to fourth-year studies) are eligible to participate in the examination program. There are separate exams for Latin I, Latin II, Latin III-IV prose, and Latin III-IV poetry. Each exam consists of 40 multiple-choice questions: 20 questions concerning grammar, 15 questions about Roman mythology, literature, life, and history, and 5 questions based on a short passage in Latin. Students are given 40 minutes to complete the examination.

Contestants may participate only at the level at which they are currently studying, and they may take only one exam. Students may not enter the program independently; their Latin teachers must submit an application in order to receive the examination. There is a $2 charge for each student taking the exam.

High school seniors who score 36 or more out of 40 points on either the Latin III-IV prose or Latin III-IV poetry exam are eligible for a scholarship. In addition to completing an application form, scholarship candidates are required to write an essay on one of three general topics and to submit two references, one of which must be from the student's Latin teacher.

Helpful Hints

The best way to prepare for the exam is to practice taking the tests from past years' contests. A packet containing a syllabus and the exams from the four previous years (all four levels included) may be ordered by sending a $5 check or money order, payable to ACL/NJCL National Latin Exam, to Linda Sharrard Montross, James Madison High School, 2500 James Madison Drive, Vienna, Virginia 22180.

Sample Test Questions

The following are sample questions from the 1983 National Latin Exam:

LATIN I:

1. Julius Caesar was a famous Roman *general.*
A) imperator B) imperatorem
C) imperatoris D) imperatores

2. Romans *used to watch* chariot races at the Circus Maximus. A) spectabunt B) spectaverunt C) spectabantur D) spectabant

3. *Vulcan's* forge was thought to be located under Mount Aetna. A) Volcanus B) Vulcani C) Vulcanum D) Vulcano

4. The name for the large area in Rome used for military training and athletic exercise was: A) Curia B) Basilica C) Pantheon D) Campus Martius

5. The goddess of wisdom and patroness of arts and crafts was: A) Diana B) Juno C) Minerva D) Vesta

LATIN II:

1. Cras milites castra ponere *will be able.* A) poterunt B) poterant C) potuerunt D) posse

2. Cives *whom* delegimus sunt fideles. A) qui B) quos C) quibus D) quorum

3. The prows *of the ships* were later transferred to the Forum in Rome. A) nave B) navium C) navis D) naves

4. Hannibal is known for his spectacular: A) defeat of the city of Rome B) crossing of the Alps with elephants C) swimming of the Strait of Messina D) sailing from Carthage to Greece in one day

5. The Trojan War began with the kidnapping of: A) Andromache B) Dido C) Venus D) Helen

LATIN III-IV PROSE:
READ THE PASSAGE AND ANSWER THE QUESTIONS.
The Gauls Enter Rome
(Adapted from Livy's Ab Urbe Condita)
Romae interim, omnibus ad *tuendam* arcem compositis, quidam seniores domos regressi, *obstinato* ad mortem animo, adventum hostium exspectabant. Galli, ingressi postero die urbem, patente Collina porta, in forum pervenerunt, circumferentes oculos ad arcem templaque deorum. Inde, *modico* relicto praesidio, ne quis impetus ex arce aut ex Capitolio fieret, quidam ex Gallis e foro *dilapsi sunt* ut in viis domisque privatis praedam peterent. Mox autem solitudine urbis territi, ne qua *fraus* hostilis *eos vagantes* exciperet, in forum redierunt.

VOCABULARY:
tuendam = protect
obstinato = determined
modico = small
dilapsi sunt = slipped away
fraus = ambush, trick
eos vagantes = them as they wandered
1. Certain elderly Romans: A) burned their homes B) went to the Forum to meet the Gauls C) warned the Romans of a trick D) had resolved to die
2. The Gauls entered Rome: A) on the day before B) through the Colline gate C) through a triumphal arch D) through the temple doors
3. Dilapsi sunt, line 6, refers to: A) the Romans in their homes B) the Roman garrison C) the prisoners of war D) the looters
4. Fraus hostilis, line 7: A) succeeded B) never happened C) was foiled D) came too late
5. The Gauls returned to the Forum: A) boldly B) after tricking the Romans C) with hostages D) frightened

READ THE PASSAGE AND ANSWER THE QUESTIONS.
Pompey and the Pirates
Cum piratae illo tempore maria omnia infestarent et quasdam etiam Italiae urbes oppugnavissent, ad eos opprimendos missus est Pompeius Magnus. Ille, dispositis per omnes maris *recessus* navibus, brevi tempore terrarum orbem illis piratis liberavit. Tum Pompeius piratas captos in urbibus et agris *procul* a mari collocavit. Nihil hac victoria erat celerius, nam *quadraginta* diebus piratas ex toto mari expulit.

VOCABULARY
recessus = bay, inlet
procul = far away
quadraginta = 40
1. Several Italian cities: A) provided Pompey's ships B) sent a request to the senate C) were wiped out by a plague D) were attacked by the pirates
2. Ad eos opprimendos, line 2, means: A) since they had been oppressed B) at their defeat C) to defeat them D) to the place of their imprisonment
3. The pirates: A) were all killed B) were all captured C) escaped to other waters D) were forced to return the loot

4. In the inland cities: A) the loot was redistributed B) the pirates were resettled C) Pompey's troops were rewarded D) a forty-day holiday was proclaimed
5. Pompey's victory was accomplished: A) at a great cost to the Romans B) with forty ships C) very quickly D) in spite of a great storm.

Program Deadlines

Application forms for the exam are sent in late September or early October to teachers who are American Classical League members. Nonmembers may write for application forms to the ACL/NJCL at the address below. Teachers must submit exam application forms by early January. The exams are held during the second week in March, with results and awards announced in April. Eligible students must submit the scholarship application in May.

For More Information

Contact your Latin teacher, or write to:
        ACL/NJCL National Latin Examination
        P.O. Box 95
        Mount Vernon, Virginia 22121

The American Legion National High School Oratorical Contest

Focus:	Public speaking
Who May Enter:	Students in 9th-12th grades who are under 20 yrs old by national contest date; U.S. citizens and permanent residents only. Also open to U.S. students abroad (in some locations).
Entry Requirements:	Prepared and extemporaneous speeches
Awards:	National, sectional, regional: (1) $17,000, (1) $15,000, (1) $11,000, (1) $9000, (8) $2000, (41) $1000 scholarships State, county, local: several hundred cash awards and scholarships (amounts vary)
Deadline:	March
Sponsor/Administrator:	American Legion

The American Legion is an organization of wartime veterans of the United States Armed Forces. Its annual National High School Oratorical Contest offers both a challenging test of a high school student's skills in public speaking and a superb source of lucrative scholarship money to finance one's college education. Substantial scholarships are also awarded at state competitions, and local American Legion posts across the country present cash grants to contest winners as well.

The members of the American Legion take great pride in the high school oratorical contest and often take a strong interest in the contestants and their families. For this reason, participants have cited the experience of meeting people involved in this program as a special benefit of the competition. Entrants reaching advanced levels of the American Legion contest have the added chance to meet students and veterans from throughout the nation.

Rules and Procedures

To participate in the competition, contestants must be ninth to twelfth graders and under the age of 20 on the date of the national-level contest (held in April). They must be citizens or permanent residents of the United States.

Contestants are judged on the basis of two speeches they must give: the prepared oration and the extemporaneous discourse. The prepared oration is an original speech taking 8 to 10 minutes to deliver. The subject must be some aspect of the Constitution of the United States that emphasizes "the attendant duties and obligations of a citizen to our government." The extemporaneous discourse is a speech, from 3 to 5 minutes in length, concerning a specific passage from the Constitution. The competitors must be prepared to speak on any one of 6 topics (which are listed in the official contest rules distributed to participants). The topic that the speakers will be required to address in the competition will be given to them 5 minutes before they must deliver the speech. Students are not permitted to consult any notes, books, or other prepared materials during the 5-minute preparation period.

The first stage of competition in the oratorical contest is at the local, or post, level. Each local American Legion branch sponsors a contest and offers a modest cash award (typically $25–$50) to the winner. Post winners are eligible to advance to the district or county competition, which sends its winner to the department-level contest. A department contest is held in each state as well as in the District of Columbia and in several foreign nations.

Each department winner advances to the regional competitions (comprising winners from several states) and receives a $1000 scholarship. Regional winners compete in one of four sectional contests, and the four sectional winners compete in the national finals. Each regional winner who advances to the sectional but not to the national finals receives an additional $1000 scholarship. The national finalists receive scholarship awards of $17,000 (first place), $15,000 (second place), $11,000 (third place), and $9000 (fourth place). The American Legion pays for all travel expenses of students and their chaperones during the contest.

Helpful Hints
Writing the Prepared Oration

The principal emphasis in the scoring is placed on the prepared speech. Several criteria are used to judge the oration; each is important and should be carefully considered in order to write a winning speech.

- *Originality and freshness of approach.* Because every contestant must speak on the same topic, judges often are forced to listen to speech after speech of the same worn-out ideas and tired clichés. Selecting a fresh, creative approach is necessary not only to make the speech dynamic and interesting but also to distinguish it in a judge's mind from the rest of the competition.

- *Relevancy to subject.* It is vital that contestants address the topic directly and not go off on tangents. Speakers are judged on their ability to apply their knowledge and ideas to the topic. In attempting to make a speech interesting and entertaining, don't use material that does not directly relate to the ideas being developed.

- *Supporting and illustrating your ideas.* Any idea you present must be proved or supported through the use of examples, descriptions, analogies, or specific data. While authoritative sources (such as scholars, statesmen, and judges) are good references for a speech on the Constitution, don't be afraid to try something different as well. A humorous anecdote or a reference to a well-known novel, motion picture, or cartoon strip (such as *Peanuts* or *Doonesbury*) can add color to your presentation and help the audience relate to what you are trying to say.

- *Logic.* The prepared oration should demonstrate sound reasoning. Are the conclusions of the speaker properly drawn? Are the speaker's ideas logically developed? The answers to these questions must be "yes" if the speech is to be a winner. The judges selected by the American Legion for the oratorical contest are usually lawyers, politicians, teachers, and business people, who appreciate clear and logical thinking. A carefully reasoned speech is essential.

- *Comprehensive knowledge of subject matter.* The content of the prepared oration should display the speaker's grasp of subject and unity of thought. An effective strategy is to stress the significance of your subject and its relevance to the lives of your listeners. At the conclusion of the speech, the judges should be impressed by your knowledge and clear thinking, but they should also be struck by the importance of your message.

- *Following the rules.* Before writing your prepared oration, you will receive a copy of the official contest rules. Study the rules and follow them to the letter in order to avoid losing points unnecessarily. In particular, be certain that you announce the title of your oration at the very beginning of the presentation. Indicate sources for quotations and cite the author's name for those of more than ten words. Finally, make sure your speech is within the required time limits. These six factors—originality, relevancy, illustrations, logic, comprehensiveness, and adherence to the rules—are basic guidelines to follow in writing your prepared oration.

"The only way to prepare is through practice, practice, and more practice. A great deal of thought and originality should be devoted to the writing of the speech," advises $2000-scholarship winner Stephanie Seminara. Describing the content of her American Legion oration, she says, "My thesis was that the Constitution is evolutionary; it is a document capable of modification in changing times while remaining steadfast to principles true for all times."

The Extemporaneous Discourse

Since the extemporaneous topics are released in advance of the competition (in the official rules pamphlet), students should prepare by researching and thoroughly understanding the topics. It is extremely helpful to study books on constitutional law or Supreme Court decisions for insights and analyses of sections and amendments to the Constitution. Recommended sources are Congressional Quarterly's *Guide to the U.S. Supreme Court* and Edward S. Corwin's *The Constitution and What It Means Today* (Princeton University Press, 1978).

A word of caution: students are in a somewhat precarious situation when it comes to preparing for the extemporaneous discourse. The speech isn't really "extemporaneous"; participants are instructed to be knowledgeable about a handful of topics. Advance preparation and a significant amount of research are needed to present an informative and thought-provoking speech. The problem is that judges are instructed to downgrade contestants if they suspect parts of the extemporaneous discourse have been memorized. All too often, judges in local contests, not having read the rules carefully and with little experience in American Legion oratory, are overwhelmed by a very polished, informative extemp on a narrow and unfamiliar constitutional issue. Thus, students may run the risk of either sounding uninformative or sounding "canned" and memorized.

To avoid this dilemma, students should do two things. First, talk with the American Legion member in charge of the oratorical program *before* the contest to make sure the judges are fully aware that speakers have been instructed to research the extemp topics. Second, prepare an outline for each topic before the competition. An outline allows for organizing and structuring your research so that you will be prepared to speak. Use the 5-minute prep period to practice delivering a speech that is built around your memorized outline. Using this method, it is possible to give a well-researched presentation that is at the same time natural and conversational. The outline approach has worked for many successful contestants in the American Legion program.

Once the topic chosen for the actual competition has been announced, contestants should focus on two vital elements in preparing their extemporaneous discourse: organization and fluency. Organize the speech into two or three main sections, each expressing a major point about the topic. Each speech should summarize the content of the constitutional passage and relate its meaning. Good approaches include describing the intent of the Founding Fathers in writing the passage, analyzing Supreme Court interpretations of the topic, or looking at the impact of the topic on American history or on America today.

Sample Winning Entry

The following prepared oration, titled "The Forgotten Bill of Rights," was written by the author of this book, who was the New Jersey state champion in the 1982 contest.

> In 1787, a woman walked up to Benjamin Franklin in the streets of Philadelphia and asked him what kind of government the members of the Constitutional Convention were giving the new nation. Franklin answered: "A republic, madam—if you can keep it."
>
> Benjamin Franklin and the Founding Fathers understood how difficult it is to maintain liberty. The signers of the Declaration of Independence pledged their "lives, fortunes and sacred honor" to defend freedom. Thomas Jefferson dedicated his life to the cause of liberty, and said: "I have sworn . . . eternal hostility against every

form of tyranny over the mind of man." But for all their work and dedication, the Founding Fathers knew that liberty would always be in danger.

Today we should pay close attention to the warnings of Benjamin Franklin. The Constitution is a magnificent blueprint for freedom, but it is only a blueprint. We are the architects of our generation's fate. It is our obligation, our responsibility and our sacred duty to preserve the liberties of the Bill of Rights.

We Americans take our Constitutional freedoms for granted. We do not realize how vulnerable those freedoms are. A nationwide poll conducted by C.B.S. in the 1970s showed that a majority of Americans were ready to restrict the basic freedoms guaranteed by the Bill of Rights. These are the shocking statistics:

- Seventy-six percent of those polled opposed the freedom of groups to organize protests against the government.

- Fifty-five percent opposed freedom of the press.

- Over fifty percent opposed the right to criticize the government.

- Sixty percent opposed writs of habeus corpus.

- Fifty-eight percent opposed the fifth amendment guarantee against "double jeopardy."

The majority of Americans questioned opposed seven out of the ten Constitutional rights treated by the survey. Opposition was particularly strong to the precious freedoms of the first amendment and the rights which protect the innocent.

Ignorance of Constitutional liberties has been even more widespread among the young. A poll of high school students conducted in the 1960s by Purdue University showed that 83 percent were in favor of wiretapping, 58 percent approved of third-degree methods by the police, 60 percent approved of censorship, and 25 percent would allow the police to search a home without a warrant.

The apathy toward Constitutional rights in modern America led former Supreme Court Justice Earl Warren to say that the Bill of Rights could not be ratified in our nation today.

Our civil liberties are constantly in jeopardy. In times of crisis our liberties are most vulnerable. The fear of anarchists led to repressions of freedom after World War I. The fear of Communist subversion in the 1950s produced the McCarthy era, during which

Americans were persecuted and blacklisted for their opinions and beliefs. Yet through our nation's history, the people have always fought for their liberties—and won.

We must have that same resolve to fight for our freedoms if they are in danger in our times. Americans gave their lives to fight tyranny in Europe in the Second World War, and our young men battled for the freedom of peoples in Korea and Vietnam. Yet we take our *own* freedom for granted, and our apathy toward the Bill of Rights is very dangerous.

The Constitution can't enforce itself; *we* must put its provisions into effect. If we wish to be free, we must fulfill our responsibility. *We are the guardians of the Constitution.* Unfortunately, most Americans don't recognize this sacred responsibility. Aldous Huxley wrote that Patrick Henry's cry: "Give me liberty or give me death!" sounds melodramatic, and instead Americans would rather say: "Give me television and hamburgers but don't bother me with the responsibilities of liberty."

Every man, woman, and child in America must believe passionately in the cause of freedom. Supreme Court Justice Learned Hand observed: "Liberty lies in the hearts of men and women; when it dies there, no constitution, no law, no court can save it."

Now, you may say, what can I, as an individual citizen, do to protect liberty in America? How can I fulfill my Constitutional responsibility and duty? I would suggest four ways to defend freedom.

The first thing we must do is to have a greater awareness and understanding of the Constitution and, specifically, the Bill of Rights. We must have better-quality teaching of the Constitution in our schools. Go to your local schools and the board of education in your town to make sure civil liberties are being taught and taught well. *We have no right not to understand our rights.*

The second obligation every citizen has is to try to elect government officials who are committed to the protection of liberty. When you vote for a district judge, check his past decisions in cases involving civil liberties. Before you vote for a police chief, ask him whether he will adhere strictly to the Supreme Court rules concerning criminal justice. When you elect a congressman or a president, vote for the person who you believe will best uphold the Constitution and its liberties.

The third obligation we have is to actively voice our opinions. If you see that justice is not being done, that the Bill of Rights is being ignored—speak, speak to your friends, write letters to the press, express your views to your Congressmen. Join or support organizations that are dedicated to defending American ideals. Don't be silent—make your voice heard.

Our fourth responsibility is the most difficult one—and the most important. *We must not try to deny Constitutional rights to other people.* It is the hardest thing in the world to tolerate the opinions of others whom we oppose or hate. But, as Thomas Jefferson wrote, freedom of expression cannot be limited without being lost. This vital principle was best expressed by John Stuart Mill, who wrote that all of mankind would be no more justified in silencing one person than one person would be in silencing all of mankind.

These are our responsibilities. The price of liberty is high—but so are the rewards. We may not have the dedication of a Jefferson or the wisdom of a Franklin, but like the Founding Fathers, we too should pledge our "lives, fortunes and sacred honor" to preserving liberty in America. Franklin said that America would be "a Republic—if you can keep it." What is needed to keep our republic is individual responsibility—if we have it.

Program Deadlines

Most local competitions are held in February. State (departmental) contests are scheduled in early to mid-March. Regional, sectional, and national contests are held in April.

For More Information

Contact a local American Legion post, or write to:

The American Legion
National Americanism Commission
P.O. Box 1055
Indianapolis, Indiana 46206

American Mensa Education and Research Foundation Scholarship Program

Focus: General

Who May Enter: Students in 12th grade; also undergraduate and graduate students

Entry Requirement: Essay

Awards: Regional: (9) $1000, (9) $500, (9) $200 cash awards
Local: cash awards totaling $100,000 +

Deadline: Early March

Sponsor/Administrator: American Mensa Ltd.

Mensa is an international organization made up of individuals who have scored higher than the 98th percentile of the general population on standardized I.Q. tests. Under the auspices of the American Mensa Education and Research Foundation, the Mensa Scholarship Program offers substantial cash awards to students based on its evaluation of competitive essay submissions. Cash awards of $1000, $500, and $250 are presented respectively to the 3 leading applicants in each of 9 geographic regions administered by the program. Many of the 125 local Mensa chapters also offer cash awards in varying amounts, with some grants as large as $1000.

High school students planning to attend college as well as undergraduate and graduate students are eligible for the awards. However, Stuart Friedman, president of the Mensa Education and Research Foundation, estimates that roughly 75 percent of all applicants are high school seniors, and these students correspondingly receive the majority of scholarships.

Rules and Procedures

The competition is based on an essay approximately 500 words in length, in which students must describe their academic, vocational, or career goals. In discussing the academic or career direction toward which the cash award is to provide aid, students should attempt to be as specific as possible; they should include in the essay any steps they have already taken toward their goal or any experience in the field that they have already gained. All essays must be typewritten and submitted with a one-page form containing background data about the applicant.

The entries are judged at three levels. Initial screening is conducted at the local level. The best essays from local competition are then reviewed by regional scholarship judges. A small number of finalist entries are sent from the nine regions to the national committee, which selects the three top winners in each region. Winners must show proof of acceptance at an accredited American institution of postsecondary education in order to receive an award.

Program Deadlines

Contest entries must be submitted by early March. Announcement of award winners is made in early June.

For More Information/Application Forms

Contact your local Mensa chapter, or write to:

> American Mensa—Scholarship Committee
> 1701 West 3rd Street
> Brooklyn, New York 11223

America's Junior Miss Program

Focus:	General
Who May Enter:	High school girls in 12th grade; U.S. citizens only. Also open to students in PR.
Entry Requirements:	SAT/ACT, transcript, interview, fitness, talent
Awards:	$2.5 million in scholarships and cash awards at all levels (national, state, local); $100,000 + at the national level
Deadline:	Early autumn
Sponsors/Administrator:	Coca-Cola USA, Inc., Hershey, Inc., Kraft, Inc., Revlon, Inc., Republic, Inc., Simplicity, Inc./America's Junior Miss, Inc.

Although many high school students may dismiss this competition as "just another beauty contest," America's Junior Miss Program is, quite simply, one of the nation's richest merit-based scholarship competitions. The scholarships that are awarded annually at the local, state, and national levels total a staggering $2.5-million, and the national finals are broadcast as a prime-time television special, viewed by millions across the country. Fifty percent of the scoring is based on scholastic achievement and interviews, and there is no swimsuit competition.

The Junior Miss Program is probably the only beauty pageant in which SAT scores and high school grades are considered to be as important as poise and appearance. Most successful contestants have strong academic credentials. In the 1983 group of national finalists, 50 of the 52 Junior Misses were members of the National Honor Society and/ or were high school honor roll students. The program should be viewed as an outstanding opportunity for high school senior girls who are talented achievers to compete for lucrative college scholarships.

Approximately 25,000 girls participate in the 1,400 local Junior Miss programs held each year. These local contests are conducted by a variety of civic, service, and women's organizations. Local Junior Miss winners advance to state competitions, which determine the candidates who will travel to Mobile, Alabama, to compete in the national finals.

Winners and finalists at the state level often are offered their choice of a cash award (sometimes in the range of several thousand dollars for first-place winners) or a tuition scholarship at various colleges and universities.

Over $100,000 in scholarships and cash awards is presented at the national contest, crowned by the $25,000 scholarship for the contestant selected as America's Junior Miss. The four runners-up to the first-place title each receive $5000 scholarships. Numerous awards are given to other leading scorers in each of five areas of competition at the national pageant: twenty $1000 awards are given to top scorers in preliminary competition and five $5000 awards are provided to leading contestants in the final competitions. Additional special cash awards are presented by some of the sponsoring corporations.

Rules and Procedures

Contestants must be girls who are high school seniors and U.S. citizens. Junior Miss contestants must be single and must never have been married, divorced, or had a marriage annulled.

The judging standards and contest format are the same at all levels of competition. Half of the scoring is based on behind-the-scenes screening of scholastic achievement and an interview with the judges. Onstage presentations make up the other fifty percent of the scoring—physical fitness, poise and appearance, and skills in the creative and performing arts. Scores are allocated according to the following criteria:

Scholastic Achievement (15%)
A panel of educators reviews and rates academic transcripts and scores on scholastic tests and college entrance examinations.

Judges' Interview (35%)
In a 10-minute interview with each contestant, a panel of judges looks for perception, a sense of values, clarity of expression, and concern and ability in human relations.

Physical Fitness (15%)
Coordination, stamina, agility, posture, and carriage are considered in an overall evaluation of health and physical well-being.
Poise and Appearance (15%)
Grace, grooming, poise, posture, and carriage are considered along with appearance, coordination, and composure.
Creative and Performing Arts (20%)
Scoring is based on originality, technical ability, appropriateness of selection and costume, and stage presence during a vocal, instrumental, or dance performance.

Helpful Hints

Among the 1983 state winners the most prevalent choice for the talent selection was some form of musical or dance performance. The majority of the girls presented vocal solos, dance routines, or combined song and dance numbers. Stephanie Ashmore, the Alabama contestant selected as America's Junior Miss for 1983, presented a gymnastic-ballet dance that she choreographed herself. Instrumental performances were also common. The musical selections ranged from classical pieces to jazz, Broadway, and popular compositions.

Contestants should not feel that they are limited to musical or dance performances in the talent competition, however. Past national finalists have presented speeches, dramatic presentations, and baton-twirling routines as well.

A number of the contestants have used their presentations to display several aspects of their creative talents. Patricia Maki, 1982 Montana Junior Miss, described her presentation as "ballet coupled with original drawings and self-narration of my thoughts: 'Send in the Clowns.' " Several national finalists in 1982 performed self-choreographed dance routines, and two contestants in the pageant used slides or films to accompany their musical performances. Susan Hammett of Mississippi, America's Junior Miss of 1982, sang an original song she had composed, titled "First Love." Taking an original approach and combining talents from different artistic areas can be a good way for a contestant to distinguish herself from the field of competitors.

Program Deadlines

Many local contests and state finals are held early in the school year. The national finals are held in June.

For More Information

Write to: America's Junior Miss, Inc.
P.O. Box 2786-AD
Mobile, Alabama 36652

Arts Recognition and Talent Search (ARTS)

Focus:	Dance, music, theater, visual arts, and writing
Who May Enter:	Students in 12th grade or 17- or 18-year-olds (as of 12/1) involved in an organized arts activity; U.S. citizens or permanent residents only. Open to U.S. citizens studying abroad.
Entry Requirements:	Samples of artistic work/writing, application *Advanced level:* attendance at final judging session in Miami, FL
Awards:	Scholarships totaling $2,000,000 (number and amounts vary) Cash awards totaling $400,000 (in amounts of $4000, $3000, $1500, and $500; number varies)
Deadline:	Early October
Sponsor/Administrator:	National Foundation for Advancement in the Arts/Educational Testing Service

Overview of Arts Program

The Arts Recognition and Talent Search (ARTS) is a national program aimed at recognizing the accomplishments of young artists and providing encouragement and support for their continued artistic development. Participants receive the opportunity for professional recognition and scholarships or cash awards based on their abilities in one of five artistic fields: dance, music, theater, the visual arts, or writing.

The Arts Recognition and Talent Search judging panel invites up to 150 of the top-ranking applicants to the program (30 in each of the 5 fields) to travel to Miami for an all-expense-paid 4-day session of master classes, workshops, interviews, and auditions; in the course of the session, participants have ample opportunity to meet with leading professional artists in their field. The cash awards provided to those contestants identified as outstanding are numerous and lucrative; for college-bound ARTS finalists, a wide variety of scholarship opportunities are made available. And for a select group of 20 ARTS awardees, participation in the program is the road to the highest honor conferred on high school students, recognition as a Presidential Scholar.

Sponsored by the nonprofit National Foundation for Advancement in the Arts (NFAA) and administered for the Foundation by Educational Testing Service (ETS), ARTS is a relatively recent addition to the field of merit-based awards programs; the program was first conducted in 1979-80. Strong financial support from corporations, foundations, and individuals, as well as national publicity and widespread acclaim, have made ARTS a notable standout among youth programs in artistic disciplines. For visual and performing artists as well as writers, it is the long-awaited counterpart in the arts to established, powerhouse scholarship programs that focus on academic achievement, science, and other areas.

A total of $400,000 in unrestricted cash grants is provided to leading participants. Those who are named as finalists receive grants of $3000 each. Semifinalists each receive an award of $1500, and Merit Award recipients are given $500. Additionally, a substantial number of entrants receive honorable mention. There is no predetermined number of awards each year; instead, the number of awardees depends on the caliber of the participants in any given program. In 1983, 124 ARTS participants were recipients of cash prizes.

The ARTS cash awards are supplemented by the ARTS Scholarship List Service. In 1983, over $2-million in scholarship support was made available to ARTS participants by professional and educational institutions nationwide. All entrants can participate in the ARTS Scholarship List Service, regardless of their standing in the competition. The ARTS *Prospectus* explains, "Colleges, universities, professional schools and conservatories, and performing companies, many of which offer scholarships and apprenticeships to ARTS participants, enroll in the service. They are provided with the names of ARTS applicants so that they can contact them directly." All applicants receive a complete listing of scholarships, apprenticeships, and other opportunities these institutions make available to ARTS participants.

As noted above, ARTS has the added distinction of being one of only two paths to becoming a Presidential Scholar. While high school seniors cannot apply directly for this highest of honors, they can enter the ARTS program in the hope of gaining an invitation to the White House. ETS recommends the most accomplished ARTS awardees to the U.S. Commission on Presidential Scholars. The commission reviews the nominees' general qualifications—not only their artistic ones—and designates four or five in each arts discipline as Presidential Scholars in the arts. In 1983, these high school seniors were awarded additional $1000 scholarship grants from NFAA and $1000 grants from the Geraldine R. Dodge Foundation as well as travel to Washington, D.C., for a week of special activities, including a special awards ceremony with the President. The ARTS finalists/Presidential Scholars also appear in a special public performance at the Kennedy Center for the Performing Arts.

Beyond the opportunities for awards, scholarships, and professional recognition, ARTS awardees are likely to benefit from the program in terms of their creative efforts. "It is the Foundation's intent to keep up with ARTS awardees, to know of their progress and development in the arts," noted the NFAA in its 1982 annual report. "Whatever path the ARTS awardees may ultimately choose, it is evident that the experience of coming to Miami and of matching up with their peers and being judged by the experts helps them discover exactly where in the world of art they stand. It also gives them a clear sense of being part of a community of young artists nationally."

ARTS is not a testing program, and it does not provide applicants with scores or individual critiques as part of the selection process. The fact that nine out of ten entrants generally do not receive awards or recognition may sound like heavy odds, but talented young artists should not be discouraged from taking part in ARTS. For any teenager who plans a career in an artistic field, preparing and presenting one's most outstanding work will be one of the prerequisites of success—and ARTS is a good place to gain experience in the highly competitive realm of the arts.

Rules and Procedures

The eligibility requirements for the program are as follows:

- Applicants who are in high school must be seniors in the current academic year.

- Applicants who have left high school without finishing must be studying privately or must be involved in an organized arts activity (such as a community arts program) and must be 17 or 18 years old as of December 1 of the program year.

- Applicants may not be enrolled in full-time postsecondary education—that is, education after completion of high school—except for those accelerated students in their first year of college who are still completing requirements for a high school diploma in the current academic year.

- Applicants residing in the United States must be U.S. citizens or express their intention to become citizens. If living outside the United States, applicants must be the sons or daughters of U.S. citizens.

To enter the program, applicants must submit samples of their work in the form of audiotapes (music); videotapes (dance and theater); photographs, film, videotapes, or slides (visual arts); or manuscripts (writing). Recommendations from teachers or other professionals and information about the applicant's background are also required.

Any eligible 17- or 18-year-old may enter ARTS in one or more artistic disciplines. The application materials for each category are different, and a separate application must be submitted in each category the individual enters. A registration fee of $25 must accompany each application form. A limited number of fee waivers are available for applicants who cannot afford the registration fee.

Selection Procedures

The National Foundation for Advancement in the Arts describes the program's selection procedures: "Preliminary evaluations of applicants are carried out at the Educational Testing Service in a two-stage process. First, a relatively large group of ARTS judges screens all ARTS applications and eliminates roughly two thirds of the group. The top third of applicants are then examined and discussed thoroughly by ARTS' judging panels. Of this group, up to thirty applicants in each of the five fields are invited to participate at program expense in the final adjudication process in Miami."

One judging panel is established for each of the five artistic fields. The panels—which are composed of artists, teachers of the arts, and directors of prominent art organizations—develop the evaluation criteria that are used in the competitions.

See the sections immediately following for specific rules and procedures for the dance, music, theater, visual arts, and writing components of the program.

Program Deadlines

The deadline for receipt of preliminary registration forms is early October. Application materials must be submitted by early November. In December, leading applicants are invited to attend the final judging in Miami, which occurs in January. All applicants are informed of their final status in the program by the end of February.

For Additional Information/Application Forms

Write to: Arts Recognition and Talent Search
Box 2876
Princeton, New Jersey 08541

Arts Recognition and Talent Search: Dance

The ARTS dance component of the program accepts applications in the categories of ballet, jazz, modern, and tap as well as in other cultural dance forms and in the area of choreography. Individuals who plan to enter in more than one dance category or in both dance and choreography must submit separate applications and separate videotapes for each.

The program requires participants to complete application forms, obtain at least two supporting statements from teachers or other professionals, and prepare a videotape showing a sample of performance or choreography.

In the area of dance performance, videotapes should include up to 2 minutes of technique and up to a minute and a half of a solo performance chosen by the applicant.

Submissions in choreography must be no more than 4 minutes long. The *Prospectus* specifies, "The tape may include solo and group work or, if that is not possible, two contrasting solo works."

Specifications for performance content, apparel, and the preparation of videotapes, along with additional rules and information, can be found by consulting the ARTS *Prospectus* for the current year.

Arts Recognition and Talent Search: Music

Entries in the ARTS music component are accepted in the categories of classical (including keyboard instruments, orchestral instruments, or voice), jazz (instrumentalist or vocalist), popular (piano or vocal), and composition.

In addition to completing application materials, the applicant must obtain one or more supporting statements from teachers and/or other professionals and must submit an audiotape of selected performances.

46

The program rules specify, "The required content of the audiotape varies according to the instrument. Works included on the tapes should be selected to display the full range of the applicant's technical skill and interpretative ability. All repeats should be omitted. Accompaniments must be supplied when they exist. Lengthy passages for accompaniment should be omitted. A composer should not be represented more than once."

The *Prospectus* lists very specific (and demanding) performance specifications for the several categories of music. For classical entries, the performance must include the works of several composers with widely varying styles. Entries in jazz must demonstrate a well-developed skill at improvisation and the range to handle selections with different tempos.

Performance tapes must be not less than 20 minutes or more than 30 minutes long, and the recorded sound should be of high quality.

Entries in the composition category must include a work for solo or small ensemble (either vocal or instrumental) and a work for large ensemble (for nine or more voices or instruments). Work may be submitted in any medium, including electronic. A score must be submitted for each work; at least one work (and preferably all works) must also be provided on tape. There are no time restrictions for composition entries.

Arts Recognition and Talent Search: Theater

Acting is the only category included in the theater segment of ARTS. Set and costume design are included in the visual arts segment of the program, and script writing is included in the writing segment.

In addition to completing the application forms, participants must obtain recommendations from two individuals who are involved in the theater and who are closely familiar with the applicant's work. "Theater auditions" demonstrating one's acting skills must be recorded on videotape and must include two short, contrasting solo pieces (not to exceed 2 minutes each, including introduction). One piece must be from a play published before 1910, and the other must be from a play published after 1910. Props should include no more than a stool, two chairs, and a table. Costumes and makeup, if used, should be minimal.

The *Prospectus* offers several useful pieces of advice for participants: "Applicants are encouraged to select material appropriate for their age. To show your versatility as an actor, it will be to your advantage to have the greatest possible contrast between your two audition pieces.

"Videotaped and live auditions will be judged on the basis of the actor's ability to demonstrate poise; control of material; flexibility; and versatility of movement, expression, and vocal and physical phrasing and articulation. In addition to these technical requirements, actors, through their performance, should demonstrate that they grasp the importance of the event being dramatized and that they can deliver it to the audience. The performance should be believable and make the audience care about what is taking place."

Arts Recognition and Talent Search: Visual Arts

The categories of visual arts that may be submitted in portfolios include the following: ceramics; costume design; drawing; film; graphic design; jewelry making; painting; photography; prints; sculpture; textile and fiber design; theater set design; video; and mixed media.

The *Prospectus* notes, "Applications including portfolios made up of any combination of the above categories of visual arts will be accepted. Applicants may choose to concentrate in one category of the visual arts, but if so, will also be required to show some evidence of breadth by submitting entries in at least one other category. Submissions in all categories except video, film, and photography must be in slide form." In addition to submitting a portfolio, participants must complete the application form and obtain a recommendation from an individual who knows and can best evaluate their work.

Applicants submitting slides must include between 10 and 20 examples of different artworks. Submissions of photographs should also include from 10 to 20 examples, none of which may be larger than 8 x 10 inches. Video and film entries may not exceed 5 minutes in length.

Arts Recognition and Talent Search: Writing

In the writing segment of ARTS, participants submit a portfolio of their work in one or two areas of the five categories listed below, according to the following specifications:

Poetry—(From 7 to 15 poems).

Short stories—(Totaling not more than 30 pages).

A section from a novel—(Totaling not more than 30 pages). The novel may be unfinished. The submission should include a statement of how the section relates to the novel as a whole.

A script for dramatic performance in any medium.

Expository prose—(Totaling not more than 30 pages). The submission should include essay-type discussion or argument written from a personal point of view. Entries that make extensive use of secondary materials or that engage in literary analysis are ineligible. The entry also must include one or more recommendations from a teacher or teachers familiar with the applicant's work.

Sample Entry

"Writing for Life" is a short essay by Charles Cohen of Woodcliff Lake, New Jersey. Currently a student at Harvard University, he was a semifinalist in the 1982-83 ARTS writing competition. "Writing for Life" illustrates the type of expository prose described as "a discussion written from a personal point of view."

Writing for Life

Why should I learn to write? Because a written work can be carried around. You can hold it, and turn down page corners into dog ears. When you read a work you can reread your favorite lines or thoughts, and sit leisurely for as long as you want with the book open to a page, and contemplate whatever thoughts the work cultivates. As a reader, you control your use of written work. Written work does not control you.

Nonprint media are not quite so malleable. The television shows what it wants to show when it wants to and for how long it wants to. Want to see it again? Too bad. Want to think about something you just saw? Think fast, another stimulus is coming very soon, followed by another and another. Want to experience the work outside on a spring day, or on a rainy night, or on the bus, or in a waiting room, or anywhere? Bring batteries.

You can write with nothing but a pen, a piece of paper, and an idea. There is little investment, no downpayment, no monthly charge. Filled to the brim with emotion, or poetry, or brilliant reason? Grab the napkin and jot it down. Don't feel rushed, you've got as long as you need. It's just you and the paper and pen, and the paper and pen aren't going anywhere. Make a mistake? Cross it out.

Nonprint media are not quite so convenient. You must have lights, tape, technical equipment and dozens, even hundreds of people, plus thousands of dollars to communicate an idea. Before you can begin, the actors must be made up with just the right lipstick and face color and hair color. You must be quick, you've got a deadline and every minute means more money spent. (Inspired? Just a minute while we set up the equipment . . . .)

Writing is more easily directed toward the audience. An author can write for just one person (Mom, Mrs. Johnson called) or for many (No Smoking). Private feelings can be shared with personal friends. Revolutionary ideas can be printed on mimeographs and placed under windshield wipers in parking lots. Got some offbeat ideas? Write them up. So what if we only sell 100 copies?

Nonprint media are not quite so low-keyed. If thousands of dollars are spent in the making of a work, thousands of people had better be willing to pay to experience it. Ratings! Ratings! Ratings! (Forget it J.B., the sponsors won't buy it.) Nonprint media are not the place for individuality or newness.

A written work is something different to each person. You may hear a character's voice as high, another may hear it as low. You may see the setting and think of a home where you lived once before, another will see something else. The aroma of the kitchen at holiday time may be that of tomato sauce to you, and chicken soup to someone else.

Nonprint media are not quite so individualized. A character looks the same to you as he does to any other viewer. (Funny, that's not how I pictured him when I read the book.) You are forced to experience the same thing that everyone else experiences, even to feel the same thing that others feel. Unfortunately, the kitchen aroma doesn't come through at all; technology hasn't kept up with the mind's eye.

Writing is something that can be owned. It is mine, or yours, or his, or hers, but not everyone's. It is something that can be just what we make it, whether we are writing or reading. A written work can be carried around, in a back pocket or in a heart, and be drawn out when we have the free time we need so much of and have so little of. To write is to give, to ourselves and others, things nonprint media can't give. Why should I learn to write? Because I'm human, and I'm too complex to be turned on and off with the push of a button.

Associated General Contractors Education and Research Foundation— Undergraduate Scholarship Program

Focus:	Construction, engineering
Who May Enter:	Students in 12th grade (or in first 3 yrs of college) planning to enroll (or enrolled) in a bachelor's degree program in construction/civil engineering
Entry Requirements:	Application, transcript, essays, recommendations, need. *Advanced level:* interview
Awards:	(25–30) $1500/yr renewable scholarships
Deadline:	November 15
Sponsor/Administrator:	AGC Education and Research Foundation

The Associated General Contractors (AGC) Education and Research Foundation is a charitable organization committed to improving the science of construction. The Foundation's undergraduate scholarship program offers valuable grants to high school seniors as well as to college freshmen, sophomores, and juniors enrolled, or planning to enroll, in a four-year degree program in construction and/or civil engineering.

Twenty-five to thirty scholarships are awarded each year. The scholarships are awarded in the amount of $1500 and are renewable annually for up to four years of undergraduate study.

Rules and Procedures

Scholarship candidates must complete a comprehensive four-page application form covering scholastic information, employment experience, and financial information (including estimated college costs). The application also requires brief essays concerning extracurricular activities and the student's interest in a construction industry career. In addition, the AGC Foundation must receive a copy of the applicant's high school transcript as well as evaluation forms completed by a school faculty member and two adults not related to the applicant. These evaluations should center on social and personal traits—such as cooperation, courtesy, initiative, leadership, and maturity—rather than academic achievement. After the applications have been reviewed, finalist candidates are interviewed by a representative of the AGC Foundation.

Helpful Hints

Carol E. Cooper, Director of Programs of the Associated General Contractors, offers the following observations:

"As high school seniors are rated against each other in the scholarship competition (and not against the applicants who are college students), they have just as much chance to be selected as a finalist as does the college student. We have found, however, that many high school seniors are disqualified from the competition because (a) they are undecided about their major; (b) they plan to go to a community college rather than a four-year school; (c) they plan to major in architecture or another major that is not civil engineering or construction. The rules are noted clearly but are not always read carefully.

"Selections for our scholarships are made on the basis of academic performance, extracurricular activities, employment experience, and financial need. Perhaps the most important criterion for selection, however, is that the student must sincerely desire to pursue a career in the construction industry. All of these factors are taken into account when we select our scholarship recipients—we look for the most well-rounded students in all categories."

Program Deadlines

The deadline for submission of application forms and supporting documents is November 15. Finalists are selected in January. Scholarship recipients are announced in March.

For More Information/Application Forms

Write to: Director of Programs
            AGC Education and Research Foundation
            1957 E Street, N.W.
            Washington, D.C. 20006

Bell Laboratories Engineering Scholarship Program

Focus:	Engineering
Who May Enter:	Women and minority students planning to earn a bachelor's degree in electrical or mechanical engineering or computer science; U.S. citizens only
Entry Requirements:	Application, GPA, class rank, PSAT, SAT/ACT, recommendations, essay
Awards:	(15) four-yr scholarships at any of 23 colleges and summer employment at Bell Labs
Deadline:	March 1
Sponsor/Administrator:	Bell Labs

The objective of the Bell Laboratories Engineering Scholarship Program (BLESP) is to encourage and assist academically qualified women and black, Hispanic, or Native American minority group members to enter the engineering profession. Under the program, Bell Laboratories provides financial support for studies in computer science, electrical engineering, or mechanical engineering at selected undergraduate schools. This support covers tuition, mandatory fees, room and board or a living allowance (whichever is appropriate), and required books and supplies.

BLESP also provides summer employment lasting for ten or more consecutive weeks at an appropriate Bell Laboratories location, where the participant works with a Bell Labs engineer.

Participation in BLESP creates no obligation on the part of the participants or Bell Laboratories with respect to subsequent regular employment. However, qualified participants will be given full consideration for regular employment at the conclusion of their undergraduate studies.

Terry Jones, administrator of the program, observes, "The Bell Labs Engineering Scholarship Program affords students the opportunity to attend the college or university that offers the best engineering or computer science curriculum, regardless of the cost. The summer employment provision provides students with experience in a business environment and exposes them to their technical field."

Rules and Procedures

To be eligible to participate in the program, applicants must be women and/or members of a minority group and must plan to complete a bachelor's degree in electrical or mechanical engineering or computer science. U.S. citizenship is also required. Scholarship candidates must submit an application form listing grade-point average, class rank, standardized test scores (PSAT, SAT, ACT), scholastic honors, and extracurricular activities or hobbies. Students must also submit their high school transcript and three letters of recommendation from their high school teachers, counselors, or principal. The nature of the student's high school curriculum is another factor considered in the selection of scholarship winners. In addition, candidates must write a personal statement of interests, answering the questions "How did you become interested in engineering or computer science? How do you intend to use your technical training?"

Students qualifying for scholarships select the college or university (among participating schools) and the specific major toward which they wish to use their award. BLESP scholarships are renewable each semester to completion of the B.S. degree, subject to the participant's continued major concentration in electrical or mechanical engineering or computer science, maintenance of a B average in college course work, and satisfactory performance during summer employment at Bell Labs.

The colleges and universities listed below participate in the Bell Labs program. Students may be awarded the scholarship prior to receiving formal admission to one of these schools. However, scholarship winners must be enrolled as a student at one of these institutions before they may utilize any part of the award.

SCHOOLS PARTICIPATING IN BLESP

School	Computer Science	Electrical Engineering	Mechanical Engineering
Brown		X	
Carnegie-Mellon	X		
Colorado, University of	X		
Columbia	X	X	X
Cornell	X	X	X
Harvard	X	X	
Howard		X	
Illinois Institute of Technology		X	X
Jackson State	X		
Lehigh		X	X
MIT		X	X
Michigan	X	X	X
North Carolina A&T		X	X
Ohio State	X	X	X
Penn State		X	
Prairie View A&M		X	X
Princeton	X	X	
Purdue	X	X	X
Rensselaer	X		
Southern University	X	X	X
Stanford	X	X	X
Tennessee State University		X	X
Tuskegee Institute		X	X

Program Deadlines

The application form must be submitted by March 1. The high school transcript, letters of recommendation, and SAT/ACT scores are due by March 15.

For More Information/Application Forms

Write to: Bell Laboratories Engineering Scholarship Program
Bell Laboratories
150 John F. Kennedy Parkway
Short Hills, New Jersey 07078

Best Products Foundation Scholarship Program

Focus:	Vocational/technical skills
Who May Enter:	Students in 12th grade (and high school graduates) planning postsecondary vocational/technical study *not* leading to a bachelor's degree; must be residents of states where Best Products Co. has facilities (see list under Rules and Procedures)
Entry Requirements:	Application, recommendations, work experience, need
Awards:	$300–$1000/yr renewable scholarships (number varies)
Deadline:	March 1
Sponsor/Administrator:	Best Products Foundation/Citizens Scholarship Foundation of America

The Best Products Foundation sponsors a scholarship program to assist people pursuing postsecondary vocational or technical study programs. Administered by the Citizens Scholarship Foundation of America (CSFA), the Best Foundation scholarships have helped people prepare for careers as barbers, butchers, cooks, data processing programmers, nurses, secretaries, word processing technicians, and x-ray technicians, among many other fields.

The scholarships for tuition and school-related fees range from $300 to $1000, and all awards are renewable annually. The number of scholarships awarded each year depends on available funds.

Rules and Procedures

To be eligible for the scholarships, applicants must either have completed high school or be high school seniors (or in a program equivalent to the senior year of high school) and be currently enrolled or planning to enroll in a postsecondary vocational or technical program not leading to a bachelor's degree. Applicants must reside in states where Best Products Co., Inc., has facilities (including Arizona, California, Colorado, Delaware, District of Columbia, Florida, Idaho, Illinois, Kansas, Maryland, Michigan, Minnesota, Montana, Nevada, New Jersey, New Mexico, North Carolina, Ohio, Oregon, Pennsylvania, South Dakota, Texas, Utah, Virginia, Washington, West Virginia, and Wyoming).

The scholarship grants may be applied to course work given by non-degree-granting nursing institutions, professional or vocational/technical schools, and associate-degree-granting institutions as well as to programs not leading to a bachelor's degree in colleges and universities.

Scholarships are awarded on the basis of work experience, educational performance, participation in school and community activities, financial need, and job market opportunities in the field the student is entering. Scholarship candidates must provide information about their qualifications on an application form. In addition, applicants must submit an appraisal of their ability and goals that has been prepared by a school counselor or teacher or by an employer, clergyman, job supervisor, or other person who is in a position to evaluate the scholarship candidate.

Program Deadlines

Requests for application materials must be received no later than March 1. Completed applications must be submitted on or before April 1. Award recipients are notified by June.

For More Information/Application Forms

Write to: CSFA
Box 112-A, Londonderry Turnpike
RFD 7
Manchester, New Hampshire 03104

Broadcast Music Inc. Awards to Student Composers

Focus:	Music
Who May Enter:	High school students or private music students under 26 years of age as of 12/31; must be a citizen or permanent resident of a Western Hemisphere nation
Entry Requirement:	Musical composition
Awards:	$500–$2500 cash awards totaling $15,000 (number varies)
Deadline:	February 15
Sponsor/Administrator:	Broadcast Music Inc.

Broadcast Music Inc. (BMI) sponsors an annual competition to encourage the creation of concert music by fledgling composers. In addition to awarding monetary prizes, each ranging from $500 to $2500, to top-ranking participants, the program is aimed at helping the winners to secure commercial publication and recording of their award-winning compositions. The combined benefit of sizable cash prizes and professional recognition and assistance makes the BMI contest an extremely worthwhile opportunity for aspiring young composers.

Although this contest is open to applicants up to age 25, high school students should not be intimidated by the idea of competing against older students enrolled in college or music conservatories. Because the judges take into account the age and level of experience of the contestants at the time they completed their submissions, talented high school students who are skilled in musical composition should consider themselves highly competitive entrants in the program.

Rules and Procedures

Contest participants must be citizens or permanent residents of countries within the Western Hemisphere and must either be enrolled in an accredited public, private, or parochial secondary school, college, or conservatory of music or else be engaged in private study with a recognized and established music teacher. An entrant must not have reached 26 years of age in the calendar year preceding the program deadline.

Contestants must submit their compositions in manuscript form; however, electronic music or other works that cannot adequately be presented in score may be submitted on reel-to-reel tape or cassettes. There are no limitations as to musical style, instrumentation, or length of the manuscript. Jointly written compositions may be entered only if all coauthors meet the eligibility requirements for entering the contest.

Each composition submitted to the competition is reviewed by no fewer than three judges. The entry must be marked with a pseudonym or other identifying mark that will ensure the anonymity of the composer before the judging panel. The only information about the entrant given to the judges is the pseudonym, the composer's current age and age at the time of composition, and the name of the musical work.

Helpful Hints

In evaluating compositions submitted in the BMI competition, the judges are above all looking for evidence of genuine creative talent. According to the official rules, "Academic finesse, while not disregarded, will be considered secondary to the vital musicality of the composer's work."

In particular, the judges take into account the following:

- Formal content of the composition. This concerns the continuity and coherent expression of the composer's ideas.

- Melodic, harmonic, and rhythmic idioms. These aspects are judged in terms of their consistency and their suitability for the composition.

- Instrumentation and orchestration. These elements are judged according to their suitability for the composition.

- Age of the composer at the time of completion of the manuscript. When two compositions are of equal merit in the opinion of the judges but there is an age disparity, preference will be given to the younger contestant.

Program Deadlines

Entries must be submitted no later than February 15. Public announcement of the awards is made by late June.

For Additional Information/Application Forms

Contact: BMI Awards to Student Composers
Broadcast Music Inc.
320 West 57th Street
New York, New York 10019

The Century III Leaders Program

Focus:	Leadership
Who May Enter:	Students in 12th grade
Entry Requirements:	Exam, application, essay. *Advanced level:* interview
Awards:	National: (1) $10,000, (9) $500 scholarships State: (2) $1500, (2) $500 scholarships (per state)
Deadline:	Mid-October
Sponsor/Administrator:	Shell Oil Co. Foundation/National Association of Secondary School Principals

The Century III Leaders Program is designed to recognize outstanding leadership skills among high school seniors. More than 300,000 high school seniors from throughout the country participate each year in this highly competitive and prestigious scholarship program. Substantial scholarships are awarded to winners at both the state and the national levels. State winners participate in the national conference in historic Colonial Williamsburg, Virginia, where they propose new ideas for America's future and meet leaders in government, business, and education.

"Although scholarships are an important part of the Century III Leaders, the program involves much more," says Scott Thomson, Executive Director of the National Association of Secondary School Principals (NASSP), which administers the program. "It provides an opportunity for emerging leaders to exchange ideas about the nation's future challenges and what should be done to meet them." Taylor Smith, the 1983 national champion, remarks, "I found the entire experience to be beneficial in numerous ways. It is an opportunity for the youth of our country to speak out and share views and beliefs with the leaders of our nation. And most importantly, the leaders *listen.*"

Rules and Procedures

Century III begins with local competitions administered by participating high schools. Any senior may enter the program.

The local competition is composed of three parts, on which each student is given a numerical score:

- A current events examination (1-15 points).

- The Century III application—a 3-page application form describing the applicant's leadership experience and involvement in school and community activities (1-60 points).

- The Projection for Innovative Leadership essay—an original, 2-page essay discussing a current problem and proposing possible solutions (1-25 points).

The student with the highest total score on this 100-point scale is designated as the local Century III winner and is eligible to enter the state competition.

A state selection committee reviews all the application materials of local winners and selects ten state finalists. These students are invited to personal interviews with the committee, after which two finalists and two alternates from each state (and the District of Columbia) are chosen to attend the national conference in Williamsburg. The two state winners are each awarded a $1500 scholarship; the designated alternates each receive a $500 scholarship.

The Williamsburg program is an all-expense-paid week of activities that is centered on student participation in seminars but also includes a chance to tour the historic restored city, to make friends with contest finalists from throughout the nation, and to win additional scholarship awards. The topics selected for the seminars are based on issues that are discussed in the Projection essays submitted by the Century III state finalists. In 1983 the topics included America's Economy, Energy and Environment, Education, Technology and Values, International Security, and the Role of Government. Each student participates in two seminars, working in groups of 17 to analyze problems and propose solutions. To prepare for the seminars, all participants are sent several books as suggested reading before traveling to Williamsburg.

The national conference concludes with a "Town Meeting," at which the delegates vote on proposals. Nine national finalists and the national champion are then selected, based on evaluations of their applications and their participation in the Williamsburg program. The national finalists each receive $500 in scholarship money, while the national champion is awarded a scholarship grant of $10,000.

Helpful Hints

The Current Events Examination

Each student entering the local competition must take a standardized, 45-minute multiple-choice exam composed of 50 questions concerning current events. Many of the questions are in the areas of foreign affairs, politics, and economics; additional questions are drawn from recent developments in science, sports, and the arts.

Participants often find this exam to be very difficult unless they have devoted sufficient time to preparation and study. A useful approach is to read *TIME* magazine from cover to cover for an extended period before taking the exam. The test is prepared by TIME-LIFE Magazine Educational Programs and draws its information from events covered in *TIME*.

The Century III Application Form

The application form is composed of four sections, each of which is scored separately. The criteria for scoring are as follows:

School activities (1-25 points): The Century III applicant should have a wide variety of interests and commitments to the school community, with substantial activity in at least several different areas.

Leadership positions (1-15 points): The applicant should have a record of meeting responsibilities associated with various elected or appointed positions held in school, community, or work-related areas.

Community involvement (1-10 points): Candidates should show evidence of some form of service to or involvement with the local, state, or national community.

Work experience, recognition, and awards (1-10 points): Any factors such as jobs, honors, or awards that indicate responsible commitment and leadership on the part of the applicant are considered relevant.

A common misconception about the program is that only individuals who are involved in student government can become Century III contest winners. Although many successful participants are involved in student council or hold class office, scholarship candidates with leadership positions in church-related groups, on school newspapers and literary magazines, on athletic teams, and in many other pursuits are also frequently chosen as winners in the competition.

The Projection for Innovative Leadership Essay

Each applicant must submit a two-page, double-spaced, typewritten essay concerning an issue America will face in its third century. A third page should be included to cite sources of quotes and factual material; footnotes should not be used.

All Century III participants are given information offering insights on preparing the Projection essay along with three condensed versions of successful essays. This material should be reviewed carefully.

In approaching the essay, be certain to select a problem you can discuss clearly and knowledgeably at a later date. State finalists are questioned about their essays in the personal interview sessions and are asked to elaborate on their ideas and proposals. National champion Taylor Smith advises, "Try to write your essay around a topic in which you have personal experience or which you are very familiar with."

A crucial aspect of preparing the essay is to stress the significance of the topic that you have selected. Near the beginning of the essay, the importance of the issue to the nation (and, if possible, to the judges as concerned citizens) should be clearly and powerfully expressed.

The Interview

Because all participants who are selected to appear before the state selection committee have strong credentials, the interview plays an especially important role in the final choice of the Century III finalists and alternates.

The 10 state finalists are interviewed successively, and the sessions are designed to take approximately 20 minutes for each candidate. The panel of interviewers (the state selection committee) consists of 5 members with diverse backgrounds. The committee often includes the Century III state chairman; representatives from the field of education, including a member of the state Secondary School Principals Association; and a high school student from the state.

In such a brief meeting, the first impression one gives is highly important. Boys should wear jackets and ties, and girls should dress in comparable attire. Despite the fact that the interview is a serious situation charged with a sense of pressure, finalists should try to remain relaxed and to maintain eye contact with the members of the interview panel while listening and responding to their remarks.

Each candidate is asked the same set of predetermined questions, with the exception of questions concerning the topic Projections for Innovative Leadership, which relate specifically to each individual's essay. Students are often asked about the activities and leadership roles they listed on their applications. In past years questions have included: "Are you a leader?," "Who are the leaders, past or present, whom you most admire, and why?," "What are the most important qualities needed by a leader?," "What is your goal in life?," and "What has been your most meaningful experience in high school?" The interview is very brief and there is limited time to respond, so finalists should attempt to be as direct and succinct as possible.

A crucial factor at the interview is to answer the questions candidly and articulately. A sense of confidence and intelligence is what the committee is looking for. False modesty is not desirable in the interview; don't be afraid to speak about any significant accomplishments and achievements you have made.

Sample Winning Entry

The following Projection for Innovative Leadership essay was written by Taylor Smith, the 1983 national winner.

The Inmate Problem

Our country is being threatened by an increasing number of persons convicted of crimes and an apparently inadequate rehabilitative process. One of the promising characteristics of the United States when it was founded was its interest in setting up a penal system whereby criminals were not only punished but also transformed from "hooligans" and "idlers" into law abiding citizens. However, our ideal penal system has failed to work; therefore, our prison population continues to grow at a rapid rate.

Due to the growing rate of recidivism, now over 30%, and the increasing number of first time criminals, our prison population has almost doubled over the last twelve years. "The Inmate Nation" grows at over 170 per day. At this rate, the number of Americans in prison, today one out of every 600, will double by 1988. Only the Soviet Union and South Africa have a higher number of inmates per capita, and the gap is closing. The support of convicted persons costs the United States $4.5 billion a year and is expected to rise to $40 billion annually if new plans for increased sentences are introduced. The cost per inmate in maximum security prisons ranges from $15,000 to $30,000 annually and it is climbing.

Prison overcrowding is becoming obvious also. Illinois prison officials plan to increase space for 1,500 inmates by 1985; however, they expect to have 3,500 additional inmates by then. Florida's prisons are exceedingly overcrowded despite the completion of a new Florida prison every eight months. The cost of increasing prison space is incredibly expensive. In a Minnesota maximum security prison the cost per additional cell is $78,300. This problem of skyrocketing prison costs combined with increasing numbers of convicted persons clearly poses a very serious problem for our leaders in the Third Century, and it will be our responsibility to find a solution to this issue.

I believe that the answer to the growing recidivism and number of first time convictions is a two-step objective for the Third Century leaders. The solution to the high rate of returning inmates lies in integrating them back into society more successfully. Instead of the traditional $100 and a used suit, an increased development of vocational training during prison terms, along with follow-up programs by organizations such as men's groups from churches who will take a personal interest, would be a much more effective way to help inmates get started again. I have participated in such a group in my church and through that have become friends with a former long-term prisoner. He is now successfully adjusting to life and work in our community.

Even more importantly, the leaders of the Third Century must take the second step by severing the inmate problem at the grass roots level. Family disorganization and disintegration cause a spin-off of hurting children and young people who get caught in the net of crime. Increased help in stabilizing the family unit in the form of family growth programs in schools and communities will attack this grass-roots start of crime. These programs will teach children and parents alike how to work together with emphases on learning skills for daily living.

We must develop more educational emphasis on morality, honesty, and lawfulness to supplement academic knowledge, thus building a solid foundation for the youth of the Third Century. For example, ethics courses will allow students to evaluate choices between right and wrong in various situations. Also, additional community programs would prevent the causes of crime in early years, such as youth employment schemes, boys' clubs, community athletic organizations.

These solutions to the prison problem are not only logical, but they are financially sound as well. Lewis Thomas said in *Lives of a*

Cell that it is cheaper to inoculate a population against a disease than to pay for the expensive treatment of its victims. Prevention and effective treatment of crime rest on the shoulders of the leaders of the Third Century: us.

Program Deadlines

Program applications must be submitted by mid-October, when the current events exam is scheduled to take place. School winners are selected by the end of October. The interviews for state finalists usually take place in December, and state winners and alternates are notified in mid-January. The national conference in Williamsburg is held in early March.

For Additional Information/Application Forms

Check with your high school guidance counselor to see if your school participates in the Century III program. If not, write to:

> The National Association of Secondary School Principals
> 1904 Association Drive
> Reston, Virginia 22091

Educational Communications Scholarship Program

Focus:	General
Who May Enter:	Students in 11th-12th grades
Entry Requirements:	Application, class rank, GPA, SAT/ACT. *Advanced level:* essay
Awards:	(50+) $1000 scholarships
Deadline:	June 1
Sponsor/Administrator:	Educational Communications Scholarship Foundation

Education Communications, Inc., is the publisher of *Who's Who Among American High School Students.* The Educational Communications Scholarship Foundation makes available numerous $1000 scholarship grants to students each year. Paul Krouse, president of the Foundation, observes, "Our philosophy involves evaluating the 'total' student." The scholarship competition is based primarily on academic and nonacademic achievement. Occasionally, the need for financial assistance is also taken into account.

Rules and Procedures

All high school juniors and seniors may compete. Students may also apply during the summer immediately following their graduation from high school.

Scholarship candidates must submit an application form listing SAT or ACT scores, grade-point average, class rank, work experience, school activities, and special interests. Approximately 500 semifinalists are selected from the initial pool of applicants. Semifinalists must complete another brief application form, which requests financial information (family income and assets, estimated college costs). They also must write an essay of 250–300 words on the topic "What has been the most rewarding experience in your life? How has it influenced you, your goals, and aspirations?" Students selected as finalists are asked to provide official test scores, transcripts, and income tax returns to verify the information they have submitted. A minimum of 50 winners are selected each year.

Helpful Hints

Educational Communications evaluates scholarship applications using a quantitative judging method that places equal emphasis on class rank, grade-point average, SAT/ACT scores, extracurricular activities, and work experience. Semifinalists are also judged on their essay. Financial need comes in only as a final factor in the decision among several equally qualified candidates. The Foundation emphasizes that many awards have gone to highly qualified candidates who did not need scholarship assistance.

Program Deadlines

Applications must be submitted by June 1. Semifinalists are notified by June 15 and sent the additional application forms. Finalists are notified by August 1, and scholarship winners are contacted by August 15.

For Additional Information/Application Forms

Write to: Educational Communications Scholarship Foundation
721 North McKinley Road
Lake Forest, Illinois 60045

Elks National Foundation Most Valuable Student Scholarship Contest

Focus:	General
Who May Enter:	Students in 12th grade; U.S. citizens only
Entry Requirements:	Application, transcript, SAT/ACT, ACH, essays, recommendations, need
Awards:	Approx. 1,500 scholarships totaling $2,039,000 National: (2) $24,000, (2) $20,000, (4) $16,000, (4) $14,000, (6) $12,000, (6) $10,000, (6) $8000, (10) $7200, (10) $6000, (50) $1400, (100) $1200, (300) $1100 scholarships State: (999) $1000 scholarships
Deadline:	February 1
Sponsor/Administrator:	Elks National Foundation

Although high school seniors may grow tired of filling out a seemingly endless array of application forms, the application for the Elks National Foundation Most Valuable Student Scholarship Contest is one set of forms that no college-bound student seeking financial aid should ignore. The Elks competition awards $2.039-million in prize money to close to 1,500 winners, making it the largest private source of unrestricted scholarship aid for high school students of all backgrounds.

The awards range from $1000 grants (given to hundreds of students) to the extremely valuable $24,000 scholarships ($6000 per academic year) presented to the top male and female applicants. These first-place national winners receive an all-expense-paid trip for themselves and their families to the Elks National Convention; they also are honored at the American Academy of Achievement's Salute to Excellence program (for a description of this program, see the Appendix).

Rules and Procedures

The Elks National Foundation scholarships are awarded to students solely on the basis of a conventional (and lengthy) college-admission-style application; no speeches, interviews, performances, or special examinations are required in order to compete.

Each application must include:

- An official high school transcript of student records from the beginning of the ninth grade to the due date of the application.

- Official reports of SAT, ACT, and ACH scores.

- An "Application of Required Facts," providing class rank; scholastic, extracurricular (school-related), and civic (nonschool-related) activities and achievements; plans for college enrollment; anticipated scholarship aid; history of employment and related savings; and an analysis of the family financial situation (to be completed by a parent).

- A statement of 300 words or less, in which the applicant sets forth his or her vocational or professional goal and relates how past, present, and future activities make the accomplishment of this goal possible. Applicants also must indicate how their past deeds demonstrate their worthiness for an award.

- Up to three letters of recommendation from people in positions of authority at the applicant's high school. The letter or letters should describe the applicant's scholastic ability, work habits, leadership potential, personality, and integrity.

- Two letters of endorsement from responsible people in the community (other than school personnel) who are not related to the applicant. They should be capable of reporting on the applicant's participation in the community in terms of work service, leadership, notable skills, and outstanding recognition.

- Copies of documents demonstrating the applicant's achievements in scholarship, leadership, athletics, dramatics, community service, or other activities.

Applicants must use the official Elks National Foundation application form, obtainable from Elks lodges (photocopies of this form are not acceptable). The form must be dated and signed by the student, one or more Elks lodge officials, and the student's parents or guardian. Typewritten applications and statements are preferred over handwritten submissions. Materials submitted as part of the application must not exceed twenty pages.

Applications must be submitted to the Scholarship Chairman, Exalted Ruler, or Secretary of the local Elks lodge. Applications are reviewed by lodge and district scholarship committees and then judged by the scholarship committee of the State Elks Association. Each state committee determines the recipients of the $1000 scholarships made available at the state level and also selects a certain quota of entries for inclusion in the national competition.

All scholarships are in the form of award certificates issued by the Elks National Foundation, conditional upon the enrollment of the student in a regionally accredited American college or university. Upon receipt of a verification of enrollment from school officials, an Elks National Foundation check for the amount of the award is forwarded to the college or university to establish a credit for the student.

Helpful Hints

The following point system is used to score each application:

Scholarship	450 points
Leadership	350 points
Financial need	200 points
	1,000 points (maximum total)

The philosophy of the contest directors is expressed on part of the application form: "Only students of outstanding merit, who show an appreciation of the value of an education and who are willing to struggle to achieve success, have a chance to win our awards. Experience indicates that students with scholarship ratings (i.e., grade-point average) of 90 percent or better, with a relative standing in the upper 3 percent of their class, and who have exhibited leadership abilities, generally qualify in the group given final consideration."

Erich Orenchuk of Brick Town, New Jersey, a first-place national winner in the 1983 program and the recipient of a $20,000 college scholarship and an all-expense-paid trip to Honolulu, offers the following advice to students applying for the awards: "While writing, keep in mind just what the judges are looking for. The judges are people. When you answer the questions, communicate with them. Data is boring; conversation is interesting. Treat the questions as their side of the conversation. And if you're a high school freshman or sophomore (or even a junior), get involved! The judges love to see it, and it's an end in itself."

Program Deadlines
Applications must be filed at the local Elks lodge by February 1. The names of winners are announced by early May.

For Additional Information/Application Forms
Contact your local Elks lodge.

Future Business Leaders of America–Phi Beta Lambda—Mr. and Ms. Future Business Leader Awards

Focus:	Business skills
Who May Enter:	High school students who are FBLA members
Entry Requirement:	Exam. *Advanced level:* interviews
Awards:	Boys: (1) $500; (1) $250; (1) $150; (7) $50 cash awards Girls: (1) $500; (1) $250; (1) $150; (7) $50 cash awards
Deadline:	Varies from state to state
Sponsor/Administrator:	Future Business Leaders of America–Phi Beta Lambda, Inc.

Future Business Leaders of America–Phi Beta Lambda (FBLA-PBL) conducts chapter membership programs to provide opportunities for high school students to learn about business and the free enterprise system. Cash prizes ranging from $50 to $500 are awarded to ten boys and ten girls selected as national winners in the Mr. and Ms. Future Business Leader Awards program. The contest begins at the district level, progresses through the state level, and culminates at the organization's National Leadership Conference, where the national finalists and recipients of the twenty cash awards are selected.

In describing his experience as an FBLA chapter member and contest winner in 1982, Kevin Gentry notes: "The program provided me with numerous opportunities and taught me poise, leadership, drive, and the skills to be a successful business leader."

Rules and Procedures

Contestants for the Mr. and Ms. Future Business Leader awards must be high school chapter members of FBLA. All entrants take a written test designed to measure a student's knowledge of FBLA and business concepts. The 1-hour test covers general information about FBLA-PBL's history and bylaws; basic business principles, accounting, and economics; business mathematics and the metric system; and information management (data and word processing).

Contestants who progress to the National Leadership Conference are scheduled for an initial interview, during which they are scored on attitude and cooperation, poise and maturity, self-confidence, personal appearance, and the ability to present facts in an orderly manner. The initial interview score and the written test score are weighted equally to determine the contestants who will be scheduled for a second interview, held at the National Leadership Conference. The final interview scores determine the national winners.

Program Deadlines

The deadline for entering the contest is determined by each state chapter.

For Additional Information

Write to: Future Business Leaders of America–Phi Beta Lambda
            P.O. Box 17417–Dulles
            Washington, D.C. 20041

Graphic Arts Technical Foundation Scholarship Program

Focus:	Business and vocational skills
Who May Enter:	Students in 12th grade planning to pursue a career in graphic communications; also open to recent high school graduates not yet enrolled in college
Entry Requirements:	Application, PSAT, SAT/ACT, transcript, recommendation *Advanced level:* interview
Awards:	(About 45) $100–$1000/yr scholarships
Deadline:	January 15
Sponsor/Administrator:	National Scholarship Trust Fund

The National Scholarship Trust Fund of the Graphic Arts Technical Foundation (GATF) sponsors a competitive scholarship program for students who are interested in professional and executive careers in the field of graphic communications, which encompasses the printing, publishing, and packaging industries. The scholarships are available to students planning to work in any of a wide range of areas—including management, design, manufacturing, engineering, and science, among other fields. The grants may be used at colleges and universities offering programs leading to an associate or bachelor's degree.

Approximately 45 two- and four-year scholarships are available annually. The scholarships range from $100 to $1000 per academic year and in most cases are renewable for the duration of study. Scholarship winners are given honorary membership in the Graphic Arts Technical

Foundation while in college, and they receive regular mailings of industry literature. Each year the National Scholarship Trust Fund of GATF publishes the résumés of all graduating scholarship recipients and circulates them to industry employers to aid students in finding employment in their field.

Rules and Procedures

To participate in the program, applicants must be high school seniors or graduates not yet enrolled in college who completed high school within the preceding four years. They must be interested in pursuing a career in graphic communications.

The student's total high school record is carefully considered in the selection of scholarship recipients. Applicants must submit transcripts of their SAT scores (PSAT and ACT scores are also considered); the official high school transcript; and a letter of recommendation from their high school principal or guidance counselor appraising academic and personal performance and potential for college success. Students must also complete an application form listing school activities, academic honors, work experience, and biographical information.

Semifinalists are selected from the initial pool of applicants. All semifinalists are interviewed by graphic communications executives in their community. The national scholarship selection committee then reviews all the materials submitted by the semifinalists to determine those who will receive scholarships.

Program Deadlines

Applications must be received by January 15. Scholarship winners are notified in July.

For Additional Information/Application Forms

Write to: National Scholarship Trust Fund
            Graphic Arts Technical Foundation
            4615 Forbes Avenue
            Pittsburgh, Pennsylvania 15213

Guideposts Youth Writing Contest

Focus: Writing

Who May Enter: Students in 11th-12th grades. Also open to students overseas.

Entry Requirement: Original story

Awards: (1) $6000, (1) $5000, (1) $4000, (1) $3000, (1) $2000, (5) $1000 scholarships; (20) Smith-Corona portable typewriters

Deadline: End of November

Sponsor/Administrator: *Guideposts* magazine

Guideposts is a monthly interfaith magazine featuring articles aimed at helping individuals to develop "courage, strength, and positive attitudes through faith in God." The magazine sponsors an annual Youth Writing Contest, in which entrants submit a first-person story (up to 1,200 words in length) about an experience that the author has found to be deeply moving or memorable in a special way. Scholarships in amounts ranging from $1000 to $6000 are awarded for the ten top manuscripts. The twenty authors selected for honorable mention each receive a Smith-Corona portable typewriter. As an added bonus, each year the entries of several top contest winners are published in *Guideposts,* which has an international readership of 16 million people. The awards and the glory of being in print make the Youth Writing Contest a worthwhile opportunity for talented high school writers. In addition, given the highly personal, inspirational theme of the program, some students have found writing the story to be a very rewarding task in and of itself.

Rules and Procedures

Entrants must be high school juniors or seniors or students in equivalent grades in other countries. All stories must be the original work of the student submitting the entry and must deal with an actual personal experience of the writer. Manuscripts must be typed, double-spaced, and must be written in English.

The scholarship awards are not redeemable in cash and must be used within five years after high school graduation.

Helpful Hints

Guideposts offers to contest participants the following advice:

"Think of an experience you've had—something that happened to you at home, at school, or at the job: an exciting close call, or a tough personal decision that took moral courage—then write about it as if you were telling the story to a friend. Don't be shy about revealing your own innermost feelings.

"Here's an important thing to remember as you write the story: try to make a reader sense your faith in God. And here's something you should do before you even start to write your own story: sit down and study *Guideposts* magazine to see how others present their stories."

Van Varner, an editor of *Guideposts,* points out in a letter to English teachers that describes the program, "*Guideposts* is looking for stories, true stories, and to us, the basic elements of a story mean conflict and change—in first-person narratives." Editor James McDermott adds, "We look for clear, thoughtful writing with spiritual significance."

These insights have proved useful to a number of students who have written award-winning stories. Several recent scholarship recipients point out that in developing their manuscripts they dealt with basic personal feelings rather than dramatic events. "I tried to show the feelings that I had toward my grandmother when she had lived with my family," remarks Voigt Smith of Sterling, Illinois, third-place winner and recipient of a $4000 scholarship in 1983. Other nonspectacular themes of winning stories in recent contests have included a boy's experiences as a Little League baseball coach, a girl's disappointment about not being chosen a high school majorette, and a student's guilt feelings after shoplifting an inexpensive item.

Although entrants may be successful by drawing from their everyday experiences, some winning entries lean toward the highly inspirational and describe traumatic or very uncommon experiences (such as helping a younger brother with Down's syndrome or suffering through a serious athletic injury). "Sometimes the winners of the *Guideposts* contest have written stories about a dramatic 'miracle' or tremendous recovery that has taken place in their lives," observes Teresa Schantz of Moberly, Missouri, second-place winner and recipient of a $5000 scholarship in the 1983 competition. "But since I have many blessings and few tragedies to recall, I approached the story differently. I wrote about having an 'ordinary faith' and how such a faith can be powerful."

Perhaps the best advice to students entering the *Guideposts* Youth Writing Contest is that one's story may concern a very common, everyday occurrence or a highly emotional, dramatic event so long as the theme that emerges illustrates faith in God. In addition, both Voigt Smith and Teresa Schantz note that they studied the stories of previous contest winners before starting work on their submissions and found this to be very helpful.

Sample Winning Entry

The following is a reprint of the entry winning second place in the 1983 *Guideposts* Youth Writing Contest, written by Teresa Schantz.

Lori and Me

My mind was still caught up in vacation excitement as I walked off the plane into the Kansas City airport, exchanged hugs with my parents, and tried to answer all the questions they threw out at me. I'd been away visiting my cousins for a few weeks.

"Gosh, it's going to be great to see Lori," I interjected, referring to my best friend. Two loners, Lori Dailey and I met in the seventh grade. We fast discovered that together we could attack life and its problems, and win. A rare friendship developed in which neither of us was the "leader" but instead we shared decisions and talents. I think our love for each other was an echo of a verse from I Samuel 18:1: "And it came to pass . . . that the soul of Jonathan was knit with the soul of David, and Jonathan loved him as his own soul."

Mom spoke softly. "I think Lori really misses you too. You see, she's had kind of a shock. There was a fire. Lori's home is partly destroyed."

Now I was scared for Lori. For indeed, the fire had all but ruined the Daileys' home. Its first flickers had rapidly enveloped the kitchen. Later, as I walked through the ruins, I found nothing of the colorful, woodsy room so familiar to me. The kitchen now resembled a tomb with its black, charred walls; only ashes remained where appliances and furniture had stood. The phone on the wall had melted, and the plastic had oozed down, desperately clinging to the wall. Lori's room had the air of having been caught by surprise. Clothes still lay where she had tossed them on the bed; it was spooky.

It was many months before the Daileys found a new home and slowly replaced the necessities. Their church and friends helped with many prayers and various donations.

Although it had been a terrible experience, to my surprise it wasn't Lori who was hurt by the tragedy—but me! A gnawing feeling took over the pit of my stomach. Though I had been a lifelong Christian, Lori had only become a Christian during our freshman year in high school. Now, because of the fire, Lori had a new-found strength that I felt lacking in myself. People's incessant interest in Lori and her needs began to irritate me. I found myself standing, puzzled, before a wall of jealousy. Could I actually be jealous of Lori's fire?

Talking to Lori one afternoon, I found that the fire had actually increased her peace of mind and rearranged her priorities.

"When something like a fire happens," she said, "you find out that things really don't matter that much to you."

Looking around my own spacious room bursting with things—records, music, a desk my father had made me, pictures, sentimental mementos and awards—I felt like a bumbling hippo wallowing in selfishness. To have these objects destroyed would really hurt me, I knew. They seemed like an important part of me.

I think it was on that day that I realized what was wrong with me. Lori's young faith had been tested, and she had come through the winner. The faith I'd felt secure in had never really been tested. Now, I found myself almost wishing that something terrible would happen so that I could experience what Lori had.

My life seemed so ordinary. My father and both grandfathers being Christians, my faith had come naturally to me. Our family had experienced no gruesome deaths or horrifying accidents. My life had been woven with the various experiences of a preacher's home—both good and bad—and they had made me strong. Or, at least, I had thought so. But my life had lacked the dramatic incident that would set me apart from the crowds of average Christians.

Everything about my life had been too simple, too perfect—frighteningly so. Luke 12:48 now became almost a threat: "To whom much is given, of him will much be required." Was the Lord going to be terribly severe with me because he had given me so much, had allowed me to be so protected from tragedy?

Then one day my dad made a statement in a sermon that helped me. He said, "The great people are those who believe that nothing is ordinary. Every person, every job, every time and every place is very special. And because they really believe this, life for them, in fact, becomes extraordinary."

It made me ask myself, "What's wrong with being ordinary?" Must I do great evil in order to come back and find God? Was my faith puny because I was reared in a Christian home with few of the labor pains of growing up in a sinful world? Was I inferior spiritually because I had no dramatic story of faith to tell? Should I be ashamed of good health and a happy home?

So, strangely, Lori's fire brought spiritual victory not just to her, but to me. For the first time I really appreciated being just an ordinary person with no exciting experience to tell. Being an average person is a great blessing. For the ordinary person can, by God's power, be the most powerful force of all—a simple life used faithfully for His glory.

Program Deadlines
The deadline for submitting entries is late November. Scholarship and honorable mention winners are notified prior to being listed in *Guideposts*.

For Additional Information
Write to: Youth Writing Contest
             Guideposts Magazine
             747 Third Avenue
             New York, New York 10017

International Piano Recording Competition

Focus:	Music
Who May Enter:	Students whose piano teachers are members of the National Guild of Piano Teachers
Entry Requirement:	Tape recording of piano performance
Awards:	(1) $500, (1) $200, (1) $75, (5) $25 cash awards
Deadline:	December 1
Sponsor/Administrator:	National Guild of Piano Teachers

The International Piano Recording Competition (IPRC) of the National Guild of Piano Teachers awards medals of recognition and cash prizes in amounts of $25 to $500 to student pianists based on competitive judging of taped performances. (The "Preparatory Events" competition only will be described here because it is most relevant to high school students.)

In discussing the value of the IPRC program, Richard Bass, a faculty member of the American College of Musicians, states, "For the serious piano student, the experience of recording is invaluable in preparation for a musical career. The professional musical world should acknowledge the ambition and ability of any student who is a winner in a competition such as this one. A winner may be able to use this success to help promote his or her career in later years, to gain eligibility to participate in other competitions, or to qualify for scholarship awards at colleges, universities, and conservatories throughout the world."

Rules and Procedures

The competition is open only to students whose piano teachers are members of the National Guild of Piano Teachers. (Upon request, the Guild will provide the names of teachers in your area who are Guild members.)

Students may enter any of fourteen events, in which they must submit recordings of four or five specified piano pieces. Each event typically includes works by composers of different periods (e.g., Bach, Haydn, Chopin, Debussy). There is an entry fee of $12 per event, and students may enter as many events as they desire.

The recordings must be made on good-quality cassettes or on reel-to-reel tapes. If reel tapes are submitted, 7-inch reels should be used, recorded at 7½ inches per second. No names of students or teachers may be mentioned on the tapes. To ensure fairness, each entry is identified to the judges only by number.

A contest judge assigns a percentage grade to each student's tape. Contestants receiving a grade of 94 percent or better are awarded a silver medal and become eligible for the first-place gold medal in the event. The tapes of the first-place winners in each event are reevaluated competitively to determine the recipients of the 8 cash prizes. These include a first-place award ($500), a second-place award ($200), a third-place award ($75), and fourth- through eighth-place awards ($25 each). Students scoring in the 80 percent to 93 percent range receive a bronze medal; students scoring under 80 percent receive certificates of participation.

Helpful Hints

Judges rate the tape performances as Excellent, Very Good, Good, Fair, or Poor in each of the following areas:

Accuracy—Correct notes; rhythmic values; steadiness of pulse; continuity; tempo indications.

Style/Interpretation—Dynamics (range/contrast); dynamic shaping/ melodic contour; articulation; rhythmic flexibility; pedalling; character.

Technical Skills—Tone quality; evenness and clarity; facility/ dexterity; coordination of hands; balance and voicing.

Although judges must evaluate students based on these criteria, the percentage grade assigned to each tape is not derived quantitatively from grades for each factor. Instead, overall numerical grades are given with some degree of subjectivity. Richard Bass, a judge in the competition for three years, offers the following insights: "Because the preparation of a taped performance allows for repeated attempts at rendering the best performance the student is capable of, the opportunity of using the score when needed rather than playing from memory, and the ability to edit the tape before it is submitted, the judges' expectations with regard to accuracy and precision are somewhat higher than in a live performance situation. Although entries are evaluated primarily according to the quality of the performance itself, the technical quality and consistency of the recording may also be a factor in determining winners.

"Winning contestants tend to be those who have prepared their performances and recordings with attention to detail. They use either the recommended edition of a musical score or one of equal or better quality. Winning tapes are characterized by good sound reproduction and are virtually free of obvious errors either in the performance or preparation of the tape. Beyond these considerations, however, a truly outstanding tape will demonstrate the student's ability to communicate musically, and an effectively individual interpretation within stylistic limitations will often be a very important factor in distinguishing first-place and other cash-prize winners."

Program Deadlines
Students must send entry forms and fees to IPRC between October 1 and December 1. Recordings must be submitted by January 20.

For Additional Information/Application Forms
Write to: International Piano Recording Competition
Box 1807
Austin, Texas 78767

International Science and Engineering Fair

Focus:	Science, math, computers, engineering
Who May Enter:	Students in 9th-12th grades who are under 21 yrs old (as of 5/1). Also open to students in PR, U.S. territories, and countries abroad.
Entry Requirements:	Project exhibit at regional/state science fair. *Advanced level:* research project abstract
Awards:	General Motors ISEF Grand Awards: $50–$250 cash awards (up to 200) Special Awards Program: $50–$250 cash awards and other prizes (number varies)
Deadline:	Varies
Sponsor/Administrator:	Science Service

The International Science and Engineering Fair (ISEF) has been heralded as the "World Series of Science Fairs." This claim is scarcely an exaggeration. Held annually in May at sites throughout the United States, the ISEF is the culmination of thousands of school, regional, and state science fairs. All-expense-paid, 6-day trips to the fair are provided for more than 500 of the most outstanding high school science students worldwide: over 300 contests are represented.

Students compete in any one of the following twelve fields: Behavioral and Social Sciences; Biochemistry; Botany; Chemistry; Earth and Space Sciences; Engineering; Environmental Sciences; Mathematics and Computers; Medicine and Health; Microbiology; Physics; and Zoology.

Leading competitors receive awards through either of 2 programs—the General Motors ISEF Grand Awards program and the Special Awards program.

General Motors sponsors up to 200 cash awards for ISEF participants. The number of General Motors ISEF Grand Awards in each scientific field varies depending upon the number of entrants for that category. Generally, however, in each of the 12 categories there will be 1 first-place award ($250), 2 second-place awards ($175), and 3 third-place awards ($100 each). Fourth-place awards ($50 each) are presented to up to one quarter of the contestants. All finalists receive silver medals, and 2 of the first-place award winners are chosen to attend the Nobel Prize ceremonies in Stockholm, Sweden.

In the Special Awards program, winners in selected fields are chosen by over 45 of the nation's leading business, scientific, and governmental organizations (e.g., General Motors, Gulf Oil, the American Medical Association, the U.S. Department of Energy). The categories for which prizes are awarded are determined by the participating organizations, which send their own panels of judges to the competition to choose the winners. The awards run the gamut from cash prizes or all-expense-paid trips to scientific and engineering installations to summer jobs. Prizes may also be awarded in the form of scientific equipment, books, and magazine subscriptions or honorary medals, plaques, and certificates. A limited number of scholarships may also be available through the Special Awards program.

Science Service, the organization that administers the ISEF, offers the following remarks about the benefits of the program: "Many intangibles are received by ISEF finalists. The opportunity to discuss projects and topics of mutual interest with top scientists and engineers who come to the fair as judges or observers is one of the most valuable experiences and may often lead to further contacts and attention from experts in the field. Becoming acquainted and sharing ideas and experiences with other finalists from widely scattered areas of the United States and various foreign countries can generate new ideas and longtime friendships. The experiences of traveling to the Fair, explaining projects to visitors at the Fair, and participating in special tours arranged especially for finalists, have great educational value that cannot be obtained in any other way. All of these experiences can be considered as awards for all finalists."

Rules and Procedures

In order to qualify for competition at ISEF, a student must first be a winner in one of the more than 300 regional and state science fairs held in the United States or overseas that are affiliated with the international program. No more than two finalists from each affiliated contest may compete in the ISEF competition.

An ISEF participant may enter only one research project, and it must be his or her own work. Group research is not accepted at the ISEF.

Three copies of a typed abstract of the research are required. The abstract should include the project's purpose, procedure, results, conclusion, and applications, and it should not exceed 250 words in length. One abstract must be displayed with the exhibit; the other two must be submitted with the entry forms for review by the judges.

Students who plan projects involving vertebrate animals, human subjects, or recombinant DNA must submit one copy of a research plan and certification from qualified scientists that the project follows state and federal research regulations. This copy must be submitted with the entry forms for approval by the Scientific Review Committee and the judges. Comprehensive listings of rules, restrictions, and regulations concerning projects are included in the official contest rules booklet (available from Science Service at a fee of $.50). All entrants should read these rules very carefully.

Helpful Hints

The abstracts of award-winning projects entered by finalists in each year's ISEF are collected and published in book form. The following collections may be ordered directly from Science Service:

ABSTRACTS—28th ISEF (1977)—$1.50
ABSTRACTS—31st ISEF (1980)—$1.50
ABSTRACTS—32nd ISEF (1981)—$1.50
ABSTRACTS—33rd ISEF (1982)—$3.50
ABSTRACTS—34th ISEF (1983)—$4.50

An excellent way to gain insights into the competition is by reviewing the materials in these books. Science Service also sells a 64-page booklet, priced at $1.00, which lists the titles of projects entered in science fairs and the Westinghouse Science Talent Search (see p. 192) in past years. This useful publication can provide students with thousands of ideas for possible science projects.

Program Deadlines

Regional and national fairs affiliated with the program are held at varying dates. The International Science and Engineering Fair takes place in May.

For Additional Information

Write to: Science Service
            1719 N Street, N.W.
            Washington, D.C. 20036

James F. Lincoln Arc Welding Award Program

Focus: Vocational/technical skills

Who May Enter: High school, technical, or trade school students who are under 20 yrs old (as of 6/1)

Entry Requirement: Arc welding project

Awards: Cash awards totaling $15,000
National: (12) $250–$500 cash awards
Regional: (60) $50–$200 cash awards; (up to 150) $25 cash awards

Deadline: June 1

Sponsor/Administrator: James F. Lincoln Arc Welding Foundation

The James F. Lincoln Arc Welding Foundation sponsors a national competition that challenges shop students to create practical, well-designed projects using arc welding. The Foundation offers 12 cash prizes in amounts from $250 to $500 to winners on the national level and 60 cash prizes of $50 to $200 to winners on the regional level; in addition, awards of $25 are presented to up to 150 other deserving entrants. Richard S. Sabo, secretary of the Foundation, comments, "Nearly one half of all the students who participate in our program receive cash awards." The contest provides shop students with a unique opportunity to gain national recognition and awards for their work in school.

Rules and Procedures

The participant must be a full-time student enrolled in a high school, technical school, or trade school in the United States and must be no more than 19 years old as of June 1 (the application filing deadline). College, junior college, and technical institute students are not eligible.

Students may work individually or in groups of two or three to make an arc welding project or to perform a job using arc welding while under school supervision. Competitors must submit written entries describing the project and how it was made; the actual project is not submitted. Entries may range in length from 3 to 25 pages, including the text, photographs, sketches, and drawings. Each entry must contain at least one photograph of the completed project or job. The written part of the entry should provide a step-by-step explanation of how the project or job was undertaken. It should be written so clearly and completely that another shop student could build the project based on the description. Contestants should point out features such as practicality, appearance, cost, and safety. The entrant's name or the name of his or her school should not appear anywhere in the written entry.

Entries may be submitted in any one of the three following areas:

- Agricultural—Any equipment, tool, structure, job, or device used for raising, producing, or distributing any type of animal, fiber, or food product.

- Mechanical—Any equipment, tool, structure, job, or device used for a metal, woodworking, or mechanical operation within a school shop, a farm shop, a home repair shop, or a business shop.

- Home and Recreational—Any equipment, tool, structure, job, or device used for any practical, recreational, or decorative purpose not indicated in the other two classifications.

Entries in the competition are judged according to the following seven criteria:

- Practicality and usefulness of the project. Decorative and recreational projects are also considered useful.

- Effective and skillful use of arc welding.

- Ingenuity and imagination.

- Clarity and completeness of the entry. Another student should be able to make the project based on the written and illustrative materials that are submitted.

- Safety. The project or job should be safe, and safe practices should have been used during its construction. Safety measures should be explained in the text and through the photographs.

- Neatness. The entry should be clearly written, grammatically correct, properly organized, and neatly presented.

- Adherence to the rules and conditions. Because contestants are judged solely on the basis of the materials they submit, it is important to fulfill all the rules and requirements as to both the form and the content of the entry.

Any number of entries may be submitted by students from one school, but no student is permitted to prepare or help to prepare more than one entry. Students may receive outside help on the project from experienced welders, but the assistance should not exceed what the students might normally be given on a regular school assignment.

Helpful Hints

Recent winners on the national level have submitted entries for projects entitled High-Efficiency, Thermostatically Controlled, Fan-Forced Stove (Home and Recreational category); Heavy-Duty 3-Point Rear Blade (Agricultural category); and Abrasive Wheel Cut-Off Saw (Mechanical category). To be a successful entry, the arc-welding project need not be highly complex or original, however, just so long as it is useful. The following are examples listed in the project literature of typical projects suitable for the contest: andirons; bag cart; barrel seed treater; basketball goal; bench shears; floor lamp; footscraper; picnic table; portable grill; post lamp; post puller; table lamp; tree planter bar; wheelbarrow, and wood lathe.

Students should encourage the shop instructors in their school to help them with their projects and to take a serious and competitive attitude toward the contest. An added incentive for instructors is the fact that students who receive first- through fourth-place national awards win additional cash prizes for their schools, ranging from $100 to $250. The instructor who has assisted a student winner also receives recognition in the announcements released by the Lincoln Foundation.

Program Deadlines

All entries must be submitted by June 1. Award winners are notified in October or November.

For Additional Information

Write to: The James F. Lincoln Arc Welding Foundation
P.O. Box 17035
Cleveland, Ohio 44117

J. Edgar Hoover Foundation Scholarships

Focus:	Leadership, citizenship, community service
Who May Enter:	Boy Scout Explorers planning to enter field of law enforcement who are in 12th grade and under 21 years of age
Entry Requirements:	Application, transcript, recommendations, essay
Awards:	(6) $1000 scholarships
Deadline:	March 15
Sponsor/Administrator:	Boy Scouts of America

The J. Edgar Hoover Foundation is a nonprofit institution, organized by the friends of the late J. Edgar Hoover, former director of the Federal Bureau of Investigation. Since its inception, the foundation has supported projects and programs that Mr. Hoover worked on during his lifetime. Included in this effort has been Scouting, with particular attention in recent years to law enforcement Exploring.

The J. Edgar Hoover Foundation Scholarships are available to Explorers who have demonstrated an interest in a career in law enforcement. The $1000 tuition-assistance scholarships are presented to one candidate in each of the Boy Scouts of America's six regions.

Rules and Procedures

An Explorer interested in applying for a scholarship must be a senior in high school and under 21 years of age. Scholarship candidates must be in good physical condition, have parental consent to apply, and obtain an endorsement from a local BSA council executive. In addition, they must be active in a post specializing in law enforcement and plan to pursue a career in that field after completing their studies.

Applicants must submit a complete copy of their high school transcript and a minimum of three letters of recommendation, with at least one prepared by a law enforcement official. Students must write a statement of at least 250 words, in which they give reasons for seeking a career in law enforcement. In addition, students must list their school and community activities, leadership positions in Explorer organizations, honors and awards, and any previous law enforcement experience. In describing such experience, they should give full details, including dates, locations, and project objectives.

Each BSA council may select one scholarship applicant. The local council's selection is made by a committee of volunteers and, where possible, consultants from the law enforcement community. Applications from the council winners are submitted to the national Exploring Division, and the six national winners are selected by a committee consisting of members of the national Law Enforcement Exploring Committee and top leaders in law enforcement.

Program Deadlines

Applications must be submitted to the local council service center by March 15.

For Additional Information

Contact your local council service center, or write to:
> Exploring Division, BSA
> 1325 Walnut Hill Lane
> Irving, Texas 75062

Jostens Foundation National Scholarship Program

Focus: General

Who May Enter: Students in 12th grade. Also open to students in U.S. territories.

Entry Requirement: Application

Awards: (200) $500 scholarships ·

Deadline: November 15

Sponsor/Administrator: Jostens Foundation/Citizen's Scholarship Foundation of America

Jostens is best known to high school seniors as one of the nation's largest producers of high school yearbooks. Students should also be aware that the Jostens Foundation sponsors a national scholarship program. Under the administration of the Citizen's Scholarship Foundation of America (CSFA), the program awards $500 scholarship grants to 200 graduating high school seniors "who demonstrate outstanding achievements and leadership qualities in school and community activities, meaningful work experiences, and academic excellence."

Rules and Procedures

Interested high school seniors may apply to the program by completing a preliminary entry form, on which they provide information about their participation in school and community organizations and activities as well as any honors, awards, or other achievements they have received.

From the initial entries, 1,000 semifinalists are asked to complete a formal application. After the forms have been returned, 500 semifinalists are chosen, and then from this group 200 students are awarded $500 scholarships. The Jostens Foundation sends press releases notifying local newspapers of all semifinalists and scholarship winners.

Helpful Hints

According to Evonne Gosselin, an official at the Citizen's Scholarship Foundation of America, scholarship applications are evaluated and assigned a numerical score, with 50 percent of the score based on academic achievement and 50 percent based on the student's statement of educational goals and aspirations, work experience, and involvement in school and community affairs. The CSFA does not discriminate in the judging among the various types of activities in which students are involved; Ms. Gosselin points out that the scholarship winners' interests "run the gamut from 4-H to Little League."

Program Deadlines

Initial application forms must be submitted by November 15. Winners are notified by late April.

For Additional Information/Application Forms

See your guidance counselor, or write to:

Jostens Foundation National Scholarship Program
Citizen's Scholarship Foundation of America
P.O. Box 297
St. Peter, Minnesota 56082

Junior Achievement Awards Program

Focus:	Business skills
Who May Enter:	Students in 9th-12th grades; must be JA members
Entry Requirements:	Business/salesmanship/public speaking
Awards:	(1) full-tuition scholarship for business or fine arts study (1) $1500, (6) $1000, (1) $750, (2) $600, (1) $500, (5) $400, (5) $300, (1) $250, (5) $200, (4) $150, (2) $100, (3) $50 cash awards
Deadline:	Varies
Sponsor/Administrator:	Various corporate and individual sponsors/ Junior Achievement, Inc.

Junior Achievement (JA), the nationwide youth economics education organization, is designed to provide high school students with a unique form of involvement in the free enterprise system. Rather than studying economics merely through lectures and textbooks, JA members have a chance to learn through firsthand experience in the arena of competitive capitalism. Students organize and run small businesses over the course of the school year. This hands-on approach is remarkably effective in building a teenager's knowledge and understanding of the business world, and involvement in JA can help a student in pursuing career interests and goals.

Established Junior Achievement programs are found in communities throughout the nation, and new programs can be initiated by local volunteers. Junior Achievement, Inc., observes, "By helping them understand the free enterprise system, JA enables teens to see a place for themselves in it. In their JA companies, these young people discover what they enjoy most about being in business—keeping books, selling, developing new products, personnel work—and this knowledge helps them in their later choice of a career. Even those who don't make a career in business become better educated citizens and consumers because of their JA experience."

In addition to the challenge involved in spearheading a JA company, students compete in local and national competitions for a total of almost $14,000 in cash awards. The awards are given for outstanding performance in JA businesses as well as in contests in public speaking and salesmanship. Additionally, the Walt Disney Foundation sponsors a four-year, full-tuition college scholarship for the study of business or fine arts.

The numerous cash awards presented to top participants at the national competitions (held as part of the JA National Conference) are as follows:

President—$1500, $750, $400, (3) $200
VP Finance—$1000, $600, $400, $300, $200
VP Personnel and Corporate Secretary—$1000, $600, $400, $300, $200
VP Production—$1000, $400, $300, (2) $150
VP Marketing—$1000, $400, $300, (2) $150
Public Speaking—$1000, $500, $300, (2) $100
Salesmanship—$1000, $250, (3) $50

Rules and Procedures

Junior Achievement is open to all ninth, tenth, eleventh, and twelfth grade students. Only active members of a JA program may compete for awards.

To organize a JA program, students form groups of about twenty-five members at the start of the program. Financed by individual or corporate sponsors and guided by volunteer adult advisers, local JA groups elect officers, choose a product to manufacture, keep books and map out marketing plans, and produce, promote, and sell the company's product. At the end of the program they liquidate the company, publish an annual report, and often return dividends to stockholders.

The awards contests begin with competition at the local level, through which winners qualify to compete in the national competitions.

Five areas of competition are based on the performance of JA program members holding the following elected offices: President, Vice-President of Finance, Vice-President of Personnel/Corporate Secretary, Vice-President of Production, and Vice-President of Marketing. The other two categories of competition are in public speaking and salesmanship.

The public speaking contest requires that participants first take a general examination on economics and business. Contestants must prepare a 5-minute speech on a selected theme as well as present extemporaneous speeches.

Program Deadlines

To participate in a JA program, students must begin organizing their business projects by the end of November. The annual JA conference is held the following August. The deadline for applying for the Walt Disney scholarship varies from year to year.

For Additional Information

Write to: Junior Achievement, Inc.
             550 Summer Street
             Stamford, Connecticut 06901

NAACP Roy Wilkins Scholarships

Focus:	General
Who May Enter:	Minority students in 12th grade or in 1st or 2nd year of college
Entry Requirements:	Application, transcript, recommendations, essay, need
Awards:	(10–12) $1000 scholarships
Deadline:	Early June
Sponsor/Administrator:	National Association for the Advancement of Colored People

The Roy Wilkins Scholarships are administered by the National Association for the Advancement of Colored People (NAACP). The awards were established in 1963 and named for the black civil rights leader and former longtime executive director of the NAACP, who spent most of his career associated with that organization. Each year ten to twelve $1000 scholarships are given to minority students on the basis of academic achievement, leadership ability, and financial need. Financial support for the scholarship program is provided by individuals and by major corporations, including American Can, Anheuser-Busch, Gulf Oil, and Pepsi-Cola.

Rules and Procedures

The scholarship applicant must be a minority student who is graduating or has graduated from high school and has not matriculated beyond the second year of college. All applicants must have been accepted or already enrolled at a qualifying postsecondary educational institution.

Scholarship candidates must submit a formal letter of application, in which they briefly describe pertinent aspects of their educational and personal background and their professional goals. They must also complete a form covering information about their work experience and college study plans.

Supporting materials that are required include a high school (or college) transcript, letters of reference and recommendation, and evidence of financial need (in the form of a statement by the student or the student's parents together with a financial aid statement from the student's selected college). One letter of recommendation must be from the president or an adviser of the Youth Council, College Chapter, or Branch Chapter of the NAACP, indicating the candidate's leadership potential and financial need.

Program Deadlines

Scholarship applications must be submitted no later than the first week in June.

For Additional Information/Application Forms

Write to: National Association for the Advancement of Colored People
Youth and College Division
186 Remsen Street
Brooklyn, New York 11201

National Achievement Scholarship Program for Outstanding Negro Students

Focus: General

Who May Enter: Black students who take the PSAT/NMSQT no later than 11th grade and plan to enroll in a bachelor's degree program; U.S. citizens and permanent residents only

Entry Requirements: PSAT/NMSQT. *Advanced level:* SAT, transcript, recommendations, application, essay

Awards: (350) $1000 National Achievement scholarships
(200) $250–$2500/yr corporate-sponsored scholarships
(100) $2000/yr college-sponsored scholarships

Deadline: PSAT/NMSQT test date (in late October)

Sponsor/Administrator: National Merit Scholarship Corporation

The National Achievement Scholarship Program for Outstanding Negro Students was established to identify the nation's most academically promising black students and to increase their educational opportunities. The Achievement Scholarships represent a combined worth of about $2-million annually. The combination of national recognition and scholarship opportunities, including grants from some of the nation's most prestigious institutions, makes the Achievement Program a promising vehicle for the young black scholar.

About 350 one-year, nonrenewable National Achievement Scholarships of $1000 are given to students annually. About 200 corporate-sponsored, four-year Achievement Scholarships are offered to students who have special qualifications of interest to the sponsoring organizations. These grants range from $250 to $2500 or more per year. In addition, more than 100 college-sponsored, four-year Achievement Scholarships are awarded annually; these scholarships are intended to cover at least half of the student's calculated financial need up to $2000 per year. The student must attend the sponsoring college to receive this scholarship.

The National Achievement Scholarship Program is patterned closely after the National Merit Scholarship Program; both awards competitions are conducted by the National Merit Scholarship Corporation, though they are run separately. It is possible for black students to participate in both programs. There are, however, some minor differences between the corporate and college-sponsored scholarships of the Achievement Program and their counterparts in the National Merit Program. While the corporate sponsors of Achievement Scholarships usually express preferences for students who plan to pursue particular fields of study, National Merit Program corporate-sponsored awards are primarily allocated to children of employees of corporations. Also, the National Achievement Program's college sponsors are fewer in number than those of the National Merit Program.

Rules and Procedures

Over 70,000 students enter the National Achievement Scholarship Program each year. To be eligible for the scholarships one must be black and a regular, full-time high school student planning to pursue a bachelor's degree at an accredited college or university in the United States. Each scholarship candidate must be a United States citizen or permanent resident.

Participants must take the PSAT/NMSQT at the proper time (for most students, in their junior year). In order to compete, students must mark the appropriate space on their PSAT/NMSQT answer sheet.

The National Achievement Scholarship Program recognizes about 3,000 black students annually with certificates of commendation based on their performance on the PSAT/NMSQT. Some 1,500 students are designated as Semifinalists and continue in the competition. The selection of Semifinalists in the National Achievement Program parallels the method utilized in the National Merit: the number of Semifinalists is prorated by region according to black population figures, with the group selected representing the highest-scoring black students in states within the region.

Of the pool of 1,500 Semifinalists, about 1,200 are named Finalists and become eligible to compete for the 650 Achievement Scholarships. (See the Rules and Procedures section of the National Merit Scholarship Program [pp. 124–126] for additional information about the selection criteria used for both National Merit Scholarships and Achievement Scholarships.)

Program Deadlines

The PSAT/NMSQT is administered in late October at high schools throughout the nation. Students must register in advance and pay a small fee (which may be waived in the case of financial hardship). Participants receive their scores in December. Leading scorers are notified in the fall of the following year, at which time Semifinalists are designated.

For Additional Information

Write to: National Achievement Scholarship Program for Outstanding
Negro Students
One American Plaza
Evanston, Illinois 60201

National Federation of Press Women—High School Journalism Contest

Focus: Writing

Who May Enter: Students in 9th-12th grades

Entry Requirement: Published article or photograph

Awards: (4) $75, (4) $50, (4) $25 cash awards

Deadline: February or early March

Sponsor/Administrator: National Federation of Press Women, Inc.

The National Federation of Press Women (NFPW) is composed of state associations of professionals employed in all phases of the field of communications. The NFPW conducts an annual awards program to honor outstanding high school journalists. Although the prize money in this competition is comparatively small, participation provides high school students with an opportunity to gain national distinction from a major organization in the field of journalism.

Each state affiliate of the NFPW sponsors a journalism contest, and the first-place winners at the state level are entered in national competition. National winners in each of four categories—editorials, feature stories, news stories, and feature photos—receive cash awards of $75 (first place), $50 (second place), and $25 (third place). The winning entries are published in the journal of the NFPW.

Rules and Procedures

Any high school student may participate in the contest by entering work in one of the four contest categories. All submissions must be the original work of the entrant and must have been published in a high school newspaper.

Entries are judged in the national competition according to the following criteria:

Editorials—good introduction; strong supporting facts; conclusion reinforcing introductory ideas; effectiveness of the writer's argument; correct word usage.

Feature Stories—interest to readers; unusual aspects of either the material itself or its handling; wealth of information; evidence of planning; clear organization and readability; correct word usage.

News Stories—timeliness and significance of information; clear presentation of pertinent facts; logical story development; correct word usage.

Feature Photos (to be candid shots of one or more people)—clear emphasis on an activity; storytelling quality.

Program Deadlines

Deadlines for submission of entries to state contests vary from state to state but usually are in February or early March. The deadline for entries in the national contest is April 15.

For More Information/Application Forms

Write to: National Federation of Press Women, Inc.
            Box 99, 1006 Main Street
            Blue Springs, Missouri 64015

National 4-H Awards Programs

Focus:	Vocational/technical skills, leadership, citizenship, public speaking
Who May Enter:	4-H members who are 14–18 yrs old (as of 1/1)
Entry Requirement:	4-H project or activity
Awards:	(200 +) scholarships, most valued at $1000
Deadline:	Varies
Sponsor/Administrator:	National 4-H Council

4-H is the youth education program of the Cooperative Extension Service of the State Land-Grant Universities and Extension Service, U.S. Department of Agriculture. The National 4-H Awards programs offer scholarships and recognition to 4-H members for their accomplishments in over 30 project areas, ranging from specific vocational or technical fields, such as agriculture, forestry, and food preservation, to more general areas, such as public speaking, leadership, safety, and citizenship. Four to eight $1000 unrestricted scholarships are awarded to winners at the national level in each of the designated project areas. 4-H also offers some restricted scholarships to qualified 4-H members. In addition, trips to the National 4-H Congress, attended by over 1,700 youth delegates each year, are awarded to winners at either the state or sectional level.

Rules and Procedures

4-H members who are enrolled during the current 4-H year in a recognized project or activity are eligible to compete for the awards.

Each competitor must have completed a minimum of one year (including the current year) in 4-H. State winners entering national competition must have passed their 14th birthday and must not have passed their 19th birthday on January 1 of the year in which the national judging takes place.

4-H members may work on projects and activities in any of the following areas:

Achievement	Forestry
Agriculture	Gardening
Automotive	Health
Beef	Home Environment
Bicycle	Home Management
Bread	Horses
Citizenship	Leadership
Clothing	Petroleum Power
Conservation of Natural Resources	Photography
Consumer Education	Plant and Soil Science
Dairy	Public Speaking
Dairy Foods	Safety
Dog Care and Training	Sheep
Electric Energy	Swine
Entomology	Veterinary Science
Fashion Revue	Wildlife and Fisheries
Food Nutrition	Wood Science
Food Preservation	

Program participants must submit records of their projects to the County Extension agent. This agent arranges for the selection of county winners and also sends the winners' records and forms to the state 4-H office, where they will then be placed in the next stage of competition.

State winners must submit a 16-page National 4-H Report Form, their 4-H story, photographs of their 4-H project, their current year's record book in the specific program, and two head-and-shoulders photos of themselves. The 4-H Report Form and the accompanying materials, in a binder, make up the applicant's record. These materials are then used by the national judging committee in selecting national award winners.

Program Deadlines

County and state deadlines vary. National winners are selected in October, and the National 4-H Congress is held in late November.

For Additional Information

Contact your 4-H County Extension office.

National Future Farmers of America Public Speaking Contests

Focus:	Public speaking
Who May Enter:	FFA members under 21 yrs of age
Entry Requirement:	Short extemporaneous or prepared speech
Awards:	(2) $300, (2) $275, (2) $250, (2) $225 cash awards
Deadline:	Varies
Sponsor/Administrator:	Future Farmers of America

The Future Farmers of America (FFA) is a student organization chartered by Congress as an integral part of instruction in vocational agriculture. The contests conducted by the Future Farmers of America in prepared public speaking and extemporaneous public speaking are part of a group of eleven national contests for FFA members (other categories of competition include agricultural mechanics, dairy cattle, farm business management, floriculture, livestock, meats, milk quality and dairy foods, nursery/landscape, and poultry). These programs commence with local or state-level contests and culminate in the annual competition at the National FFA Convention in Kansas City, Missouri. The two public speaking contests are unique among the FFA programs in two ways: each focuses on individual competition rather than group or team efforts, and each offers cash awards to the four top winners at the national level. The cash prizes both for Prepared Public Speaking and for Extemporaneous Public Speaking are $300 for first place, $275 for second place, $250 for third place, and $225 for fourth place.

Rules and Procedures

Participation in the extemporaneous and prepared public speaking contests is restricted to FFA members who are under 21 years of age. Preliminary contests are held at the local, sectional, state, tristate, and regional levels. The national contest is limited to participation by the winners in each of the four regions:

Central Region (12 states)
Eastern Region (15 states)
Southern Region (9 states plus Puerto Rico)
Western Region (15 states)

Future Farmers of America provides national contestants with small cash grants to help cover travel expenses to Kansas City for the finals competition.

For the Prepared Public Speaking contest, participants may choose to speak on any subject that is agricultural in character and of general interest to the public. Each contestant must prepare and send in advance a written copy of the speech, including a bibliography. The speech must take from 6 to 8 minutes to deliver. Contestants are allowed an additional 5 minutes in which to respond to questions relating to the speech.

In the extemporaneous speaking competition, contestants draw three specific topics relating to vocational agriculture or to the industry of agriculture generally. They then select one of the three topics and have 30 minutes to prepare a 4- to 6-minute speech.

During the 30-minute preparation time, contestants may make notes on index cards to use while delivering their speeches. Although they may receive no outside assistance while preparing to speak, contestants are allowed to bring along up to 5 items containing reference materials for use during the preparation period. Contest officials screen all reference items, which must be printed materials (such as books and magazines); prepared notes and speeches are not permitted. To be counted as one item, a notebook of collected materials may contain up to 20 separate items totaling no more than 100 pages.

Helpful Hints

To obtain information pertaining to agriculture that can be used for research or reference in preparing for the competition, contestants should write to the United States Department of Agriculture, Washington, D.C. 20250, and to the Superintendent of Documents, U.S. Government Printing Office, Washington, D.C. 20402.

Program Deadlines

Local, state, and regional contest schedules vary. The national contest in Kansas City is held in November.

For Additional Information

Contact local or state FFA directors, or write to:

> National FFA Center
> 5632 Mt. Vernon Memorial Highway
> P.O. Box 15160
> Alexandria, Virginia 22309

National History Day

Focus:	History
Who May Enter:	Students in 6th-12th grades
Entry Requirement:	Research paper or project, live performance, or media presentation
Awards:	National: (12) $1000, (12) $500, (12) $200 cash awards; additional special cash awards (number and amounts vary) State and district: certificates, medals, and trophies
Deadline:	Varies
Sponsor/Administrator:	National History Day, Inc.

National History Day is a program of local and state-level history contests culminating in a national competition, held in the Washington, D.C., area. High school and junior high school students compete for cash prizes and recognition based on research papers, projects, live performances, and media presentations they prepare on a selected historical theme. The National History Day program has received considerable attention and acclaim from the media and the educational community, and in 1983 it drew over 100,000 entrants. Contests are now held in 40 states and the District of Columbia, and there are plans to expand the program nationwide in the near future.

Separate competitions are held for Junior Division entrants (grades 6-8) and Senior Division entrants (grades 9-12) in six contest categories: Historical Paper, Individual Project, Group Project, Individual

Performance, Group Performance, and Media Presentation (Individual or Group).

District and state-level contests are held on college campuses or at historical societies. The two top state winners in each event and age division advance to the national competition, which is held at the University of Maryland at College Park in mid-June.

At the national contest, monetary awards of $1000 (first place), $500 (second place), and $200 (third place) are given to Junior and Senior Division winners in each of the six events. Special cash awards on the national level are also given in selected areas, including women's history, labor history, naval history, and American agricultural history. Awards on the district and state levels include certificates, medals, and trophies.

Rules and Procedures

Any sixth through twelfth grade student attending school in a state where the contest is being held may participate in National History Day. Contest entries are judged in relation to the theme of the year's program, and each must demonstrate original historical research. Past themes have included "Trade and Industry in History" and "Turning Points in History: People, Ideas, Events." No student may submit (or perform) more than one entry per year, and all participants must personally attend the contest. Historical papers must be the work of a single student; group projects are limited to five students.

The entries are evaluated by high school social studies teachers, college and university history professors, historical society officials, and members of the community with an educational background in the field. Scores are assigned according to the following criteria: Historical Quality (60 percent), Quality of Presentation (20 percent), and Adherence to Theme and Rules (20 percent).

Historical Papers

Papers must be between 1,000 and 2,500 words long, excluding footnotes and bibliography. In addition to essays and other forms of discursive writing, poetry, diaries, and fictional accounts may be submitted provided they are based on documented historical fact.

Projects

A project may take the form of a display; a pictorial, overlay, or relief map; a reconstruction; a chart; or a model. Photographic presentations accompanied by explanatory text are also suitable. A description of the methods of research and of construction together with a brief bibliography (typewritten or legibly handwritten) must accompany the project.

Performances

Performances may take the form of a lecture, demonstration, or dramatization—including pantomimes, puppet shows, or dramatic readings. Anything that can be delivered in front of an audience is suitable. A live performance may be accompanied by slides or a tape recording. Students may make full use of costumes, equipment, scenery, and scripts. Presentations are limited to 10 minutes' running time, and students are allowed 5 minutes to set up props and 5 minutes to remove them. All performances must include three copies of a brief (one-page) typewritten or legibly handwritten bibliography and description of the methods for researching and developing the entry.

Media Presentations

A media entry is a performance that is developed in slide and tape form, as a motion picture, or as a videotape. From one to five students may work on media presentations. Entrants plan and direct the presentation and run all equipment used to produce the entry. The same regulations as to running time and required written submissions that apply to performances also apply to media presentations.

Helpful Hints

A 21-page booklet, the National History Day Teacher/Student Guide, is sent to both high school and junior high school history or social studies teachers early in the academic year. This booklet announces the theme of the contest and provides much valuable information to aid students in preparing their entries. Students who are interested in participating in the National History Day program should request a copy of the complete contents of the guide from their teachers.

The annual theme for the program is usually very broad, and students may have difficulty in selecting a specific topic for their entries. The booklet gives sample suggestions of topics that offer a good perspective on the various approaches students may take. For the "Turning Points in History" theme, for example, suggested topics included: Mahatma Gandhi and Passive Resistance; Marco Polo Visits China; The Introduction of the Equal Rights Amendment in 1923; A New Industry Begins; and Julius Caesar is Assassinated. The booklet also contains much advice on how to go about researching a topic, including a comprehensive bibliography of general works that may be helpful to students.

Excerpts from Winning Entries

The first-, second-, and third-place winning entries in the Historical Paper category (Senior Division) of the 1982 National History Day program illustrate several successful approaches students have taken in selecting a topic and developing it into a prize-winning paper.

Anne Mullen of St. Catherine's School in Richmond, Virginia, won first place in the competition with a paper titled "Three Examples of Mercantilism." Mercantilism was one of the suggested topics listed in the Teacher/Student Guide for the 1982 program. Anne Mullen wrote a lengthy, well-documented paper viewing the subject from three historical standpoints. The paper begins:

> At first glance, it would seem almost ludicrous to propose that mercantilist policies, so thoroughly divorced from the American economy in time and political context, could ever have played a part in the formation of the United States' economic establishment. However, various facets of these same policies have resurfaced from time to time throughout American history sporting new names and intended for different purposes. The mercantilist hailed government intervention as the ultimate cure for economic ills and, needless to say, a similar attitude has been espoused by many prominent Americans and influential foreigners.
>
> This basic principle has been well illustrated in three divergent areas: Alexander Hamilton's *Report on Manufacturers,* the Keynesian prescription for economic problems in the United States, and a number of theories and procedures on how to strengthen the economy propounded during the last few years. Of course, the mercantilists' objectives differed greatly from those of Hamilton, Keynes, and the modern economic theorists, but in many cases the result was the same, an escalation of government involvement in the economic system. Hamilton hoped to build up a vulnerable new country; Keynes sought a cure for unemployment and inflation; and recent policy-makers have attempted and are still attempting to bolster a weakening economy undermined by "stagflation."

From the beginning, the subject of the paper is carefully defined and clearly stated. The paper continues with a thorough examination of mercantilist theory, the ideas of Hamilton and Keynes, and recent economic policies, all placed in a historical context. The author concludes:

Unfortunately, the systems devised by these economists had their faults. In particular, the emphasis on society as the determinant of economic policy instead of the individual could be cited as a major error in each. Under Hamiltonian, Keynesian, and recent policies, the American citizen was and is excluded more and more from the economic process.

In conclusion, the point can be made that no economic theory may ever be considered dead or obsolete. Mercantilism, itself, reappeared where it was least expected and exercised a profound influence on a society which would never have admitted to being mercantilist in any sense of the word. Times, governments, and people may change, but the patterns of man's economic activities appear to repeat themselves again and again.

The paper is well reasoned and scholarly, written as though it would be submitted in a college course on economic history. The subject matter is challenging; the ideas that are discussed are complex; and the tone of the paper is erudite and objective. The entry is probably most skillful in the area of "historical quality": an idea is traced throughout the course of American history, with important conclusions drawn about history in general as well as about specific theories.

William Farr of North County High School in Bonne Terre, Missouri, took a different approach for his paper, which won second place in national competition. Entitled "Planks for Industry," the entry begins:

This is a story of a plank road built in the State of Missouri, and its effects on the surrounding area. I intend to show that because of this road, the mining industry developed quickly and so did the Mineral Area of Missouri.

Transportation, according to Rudyard Kipling, is civilization. It is true that transportation facilities have always been a vital part of the development of industry. The plank road that was built between St. Genevieve and Iron Mountain was the only means by which industrialization came to the Mineral Area of Missouri as soon as it did. River transportation played only a secondary part in the development, and the railroads had not yet been brought into the area. Prior to the 1840s inland transportation of goods and raw materials throughout Missouri was limited to mule and horse-drawn wagons over rutted, dirt roads. In good weather travel was difficult, in rainy weather or winter weather, travel was impossible.

While Anne Mullen examined issues of national concern, William Farr used his paper to study a subject of historical importance to a region in Missouri. The purpose and direction of the paper is immediately and clearly defined. Although the entry concerns the history of a single region, it also sheds light on the development of transportation in general. The paper is documented with information from books and periodicals from the 19th century as well as recent publications.

David Risser of Woodrow Wilson High School in Washington, D.C., won third place in the 1982 National History Day contest with a paper titled "Rich's: A Shoe Store in Step." His paper begins:

> Over 115 years ago, Max Rich immigrated to the United States from Austria. In 1869 he opened a store which has developed and expanded for 113 years, yet remained under the ownership and management of a single family. The store is now one of only three or four shoe stores in the United States to be in business for this long under a single family.

The paper then covers 100 years of the history of the shoe store, drawing on information from personal interviews with members of the Rich family in addition to published materials. The text is lively reading, and in tracing the history of a shoe store, it offers interesting information about the history of Washington, D.C. David Risser writes:

> As the store became more famous, Herbert's customers included President Theodore Roosevelt, who bought hunting boots from Rich's, President Truman, Warren G. Harding, and other government officials. Herbert was largely responsible for the installation of air conditioners, to make Rich's the first multistory air-conditioned store in Washington. In fact, Herbert managed to get air conditioners in the same year the Supreme Court did in the 1930s.

By tracing the development of a single private business over the course of a century, the paper reveals the changing shape of trade and industry in America and thus demonstrates an effective way to approach the contest theme.

These three winning entries display several common strengths that contributed to their success. Although each paper tackles a subject of different scope (national, regional, and local history), the authors all transcend the specific theme they have chosen to shed light on a broader historical issue. Each contestant uses highly appropriate sources of information—whether a text from a leading economist, a business document from the 1850s, or a scrapbook clipping from a local resident.

The writing is organized and fluent, the subjects clearly defined. These award-winning papers illustrate that contestants can be successful with a variety of approaches if they pay close attention to the rules and guidelines of the National History Day competition.

Program Deadlines

Deadlines for district and state contests vary. Teachers receive information about contest dates from the contest coordinators. State historical societies are often involved in the program and may be able to provide information on local deadlines. The national contest is held in June.

For Additional Information

See your history or social studies teacher, or write to:
> National History Day, Inc.
> 11201 Euclid Avenue
> Cleveland, Ohio 44106

National Honor Society Scholarship Awards Program

Focus: General

Who May Enter: Students in 12th grade; NHS members only

Entry Requirements: Application, class rank, GPA, writing sample, transcript

Awards: (250) $1000 scholarships

Deadline: February

Sponsor/Administrator: National Association of Secondary School Principals/Educational Testing Service

Now in its fourth decade, the National Honor Society (NHS) Scholarship Awards Program offers $1000 merit-based scholarships to 250 of the most outstanding candidates from the NHS membership. The National Association of Secondary School Principals (NASSP) is the parent organization of the NHS and the sponsor of the scholarship program. Students are considered for scholarships on a state-by-state basis, with the number of awards given to students in each state based on the number of NHS chapters and members in that state.

Each NHS chapter participating in the scholarship program may nominate two chapter members who demonstrate outstanding leadership, scholarship, character, and service. Nominations are not based on any one of these factors. Instead, chapters are instructed to select students outstanding in all four qualities.

Rules and Procedures

To participate in the scholarship competition, National Honor Society members must be in the twelfth grade and must be nominated by their high school chapter of NHS. Each chapter is free to set up its own procedure for selecting scholarship nominees, although a recommended procedure, described in the Helpful Hints section below, is sent by the NASSP to all National Honor Society advisers. Although students cannot enter the contest by their own efforts directly, they can take an active role in ensuring that their candidacy will be at least considered by following this procedure.

The two nominees from each chapter are considered semifinalists in the program. Each must complete a comprehensive, six-page application form called the Scholarship Selection Questionnaire. This questionnaire requires information about the student's academic record (including grade-point average and class rank); involvement and leadership in school clubs, activities, and sports; work experience; personal activities; and honors and special recognitions. General information as to the type (public or private) and size of the school attended by the applicant is required as well. Applicants must also submit a short essay on a required topic as part of the application procedure.

A guidance counselor or teacher must write a recommendation for the applicant. A high school transcript and a $2.50 fee must accompany each Scholarship Selection Questionnaire.

The completed applications are sent to Educational Testing Service (the program administrator), which receives approximately 13,000 nominations in the NHS Scholarship Program each year. Each application is screened and methodically given a numerical score based on information contained in the Scholarship Selection Questionnaire, in particular the sections on class rank, school-related and extracurricular activities, and work experience.

The applications of high-scoring candidates are forwarded to the National Council of the NHS for the final selection of scholarship winners. At this stage the entire application is reviewed, including the essay, teacher recommendation, and other factors not evaluated by ETS. The essay and recommendation weigh heavily in the final evaluation. Thus, while the initial screening appears to be highly quantitative, the final review is equally qualitative in evaluating the student's credentials.

The scholarship stipend awarded to the 250 top competitors is sent to the college in the student's freshman year but need not be totally used in that year. The distribution of the scholarship money is decided jointly by the student and the school.

Helpful Hints

Any student who is interested in applying for the scholarships should urge the NHS adviser to use the procedures recommended by the

NASSP to select the chapter's nominees. The key points of the recommended nomination procedures are as follows:

- A scholarship review committee should be selected, composed of students (other than seniors), faculty, administrators, and community leaders.

- The committee should distribute copies of the official Scholarship Selection Questionnaire and request that all interested, eligible members complete the form and return it to the committee in advance of the program deadline.

- The committee should review the questionnaires and nominate the two seniors considered to best represent the chapter based on information on the questionnaire.

- After the nominees have been selected, the chapter adviser should assist them in completing the official printed Scholarship Selection Questionnaire to be certain that all pertinent information has been included.

The recommended model is designed to ensure that the nominees are selected fairly and objectively based on their competitiveness in the scholarship program. If an NHS chapter does not adopt this system (or a similar one using an independent review committee), a variety of problems and conflicts may result. Sometimes the decision is placed in the hands of the faculty adviser or the NHS membership (by voting); when this occurs, popularity or high school politics may come into play. For example, if the school valedictorian or NHS president is automatically selected without consideration of other National Honor Society members, the best all-around candidate may not have been selected. Students should bear in mind that the NHS scholarships are awarded for a broad spectrum of achievements and qualifications, not just those of scholarship or leadership. Because the NASSP model is aimed at removing bias and politics from the process, participants in the program should insist that this method be used at their school.

Program Deadlines

Application materials are sent to NHS advisers in December. All materials must be received by ETS in early February.

For Additional Information

Contact the NHS adviser at your school, or write to:

> National Honor Society
> NASSP Division of Student Activities
> 1904 Association Drive
> Reston, Virginia 22091

National Merit Scholarship Program

Focus:	General
Who May Enter:	Students who take the PSAT/NMSQT no later than 11th grade and plan to enroll in a bachelor's degree program; U.S. citizens and permanent residents only. Open to American students in PR, U.S. territories, and schools abroad.
Entry Requirements:	PSAT/NMSQT. *Advanced level:* SAT, transcript, recommendations, application, essay
Awards (1983-84):	(1,800) $1000 National Merit Scholarships (1,500) $250–$4000/yr corporate-sponsored scholarships (2,000) $250–$2000/yr college-sponsored scholarships
Deadline:	PSAT/NMSQT test date (in late October)
Sponsor/Administrator:	National Merit Scholarship Corporation

To thousands of high school students, parents, teachers, guidance counselors, and college officials, the concept of merit-based college scholarships instantly brings to mind the National Merit Scholarship Program—and with good reason. National Merit is the largest and most widely known private scholarship program for undergraduate study, offering college money to several thousand of the nation's most outstanding students each year. The sum total of the $1000 National Merit Scholarship awards—for which all leading participants are eligible—reaches over $1.5-million annually; corporate-sponsored and college-sponsored scholarships given to National Merit finalists exceeded a staggering $21-million in 1982. More than one million high school students enter the program each year when they take the Preliminary Scholastic Aptitude Test/National Merit Scholarship Qualifying Test (PSAT/NMSQT). Only the students who represent the upper one half of one percent of high school graduates in each state are selected as Semifinalists, and thereby become eligible to continue in the competition for lucrative scholarship opportunities.

The importance of the PSAT/NMSQT should not be underestimated by students—but very often it is. Because they are ignorant of the meaning of the strange acronym NMSQT, many high school juniors view the PSAT/NMSQT as just a "practice" for the all-important and much dreaded SAT. Yet for the student with motivation and well-developed skills in English and math, the PSAT is potentially the more crucial of the two aptitude tests. Success on the PSAT/NMSQT is the essential first step toward qualifying for a National Merit Scholarship. Achieving Semifinalist or Commended Student status alone can be a valuable credential for college admission, while program participants who become National Merit Finalists can expect to be highly sought after by the nation's leading schools. An added benefit of taking part in the program is that the names of Semifinalists are automatically reported to all American colleges and universities nationwide.

Three types of scholarships are awarded through the program. Currently, 1,800 one-time $1000 National Merit Scholarships are given to students annually. Nearly 1,500 corporate-sponsored four-year Merit Scholarships are awarded in amounts that usually range from $250 to $2000 per academic year (though some awards are as high as $4000 per year). These grants are usually reserved for children of employees of sponsoring corporations. Approximately 185 colleges and universities offer college-sponsored four-year Merit Scholarships, which cover at least half of a student's calculated financial need up to $2000 per year. A student must attend a sponsoring college to receive one of these scholarships.

Rules and Procedures

To be eligible to compete in the program one must be a regular, full-time high school student planning to pursue a bachelor's degree at an accredited college or university in the United States. Each participant must be a U.S. citizen or permanent resident. High school students are eligible to participate in the National Merit Program only if they take the

PSAT/NMSQT at the appropriate time. For those who are following a conventional, four-year academic program, this is in the eleventh grade. (Different standards may apply to students graduating early from high school.)

Performance on the PSAT/NMSQT is calculated into separate scores for the math and verbal sections. The National Merit competition is based on a selection index of twice the verbal score added to the math score. Of the 50,000 participants with the highest indexes, approximately the 15,000 highest scorers are designated as Semifinalists and continue in the competition. Letters of Commendation are sent to the remaining 35,000 students in this group.

Semifinalists are selected using a state-by-state allocation system. The number of Semifinalists in each state is about half of one percent of the graduating senior class. Thus, the selection index required to achieve Semifinalist standing varies from state to state. Additional Semifinalists are named from American schools outside state borders (including the District of Columbia, U.S. territories, and schools abroad) and from independent boarding schools that draw students from a wide geographic area.

The road to a Merit Scholarship continues for the highly select group of Semifinalists. Students must complete the Semifinalist Application provided by NMSC. It includes an essay concerning the applicant's interests and goals as well as general background data. Successful candidates must demonstrate academic excellence throughout their high school careers and receive high scores on the SAT. They must also be endorsed by the high school principal.

About ninety percent of the pool of Semifinalists fulfill the requirements and are designated as Finalists, thus becoming eligible for the three types of awards: National Merit, corporate-sponsored, and college-sponsored scholarships.

$1000 National Merit Scholarships

As in the state-by-state procedure used to designate Semifinalists, winners of $1000 National Merit Scholarships are chosen on a state representational basis, and each state's allocation is proportional to its percentage of the total number of graduates of U.S. high schools. The scholarship winners are selected from among Finalists in the competition by a committee of college admissions officers and high school guidance counselors, who review the materials submitted in conjunction with each Finalist's application. The committee's judgments are based on the candidate's academic accomplishments (including course load and difficulty of curriculum as well as grades earned);

personal qualities (such as leadership); extracurricular activities; scores on both the PSAT/NMSQT and SAT; and the official recommendation of the student by a high school official. Need is not considered for these scholarships. The committee selects winners who in the committee's judgment have the greatest potential for success during and after college.

Corporate-sponsored Scholarships

Over 400 corporations and other private organizations sponsor four-year Merit Scholarships for those who have achieved Finalist status. The sponsors themselves set the preferential criteria for the awards. Most commonly, the corporate-sponsored scholarships are reserved for Finalists who are children of employees of the sponsoring organization. Less often, the scholarships are given to students living in the geographic area where the corporation is based or to students pursuing studies in a particular field. Often a corporation will allocate funding to give a certain number of Merit Scholarships to students each year. In the event that there are not enough eligible Finalists to accept all the awards, students placing below the Finalist level are considered. These special scholarships are an added bonus of the program and account for over 800 awards each year.

College-sponsored Scholarships

In an effort to attract the highest-caliber students for enrollment at their campuses, many colleges and universities—both public and private—support Merit Scholarship programs. To win such scholarships directly from colleges and universities, Finalists may designate as their "first choice" one institution that sponsors Merit Scholarships. Each scholarship-sponsoring college or university selects winners according to its own criteria. College-sponsored four-year scholarships range from $250 to $2000 per year. Often these Merit Scholarships are provided to students as part of a larger financial-aid package that may include loans, campus employment, and grants. In this case, the Merit Scholarship must account for at least half of the student's calculated financial need up to $2000.

Helpful Hints

The National Merit competition begins with the PSAT/NMSQT, a shortened (and slightly less challenging) version of the Scholastic Aptitude Test. The verbal and mathematics sections are each scored on a scale of 20 to 80 points (resembling the SAT range of 200-800), with the verbal score doubled in computing the selection index. The highest possible selection index, then, is 240 (80 for math, 160 for verbal). Very few students perform this well, and the cut-off score for Semifinalist recognition usually runs from the low 190s to around 200.

Because it is weighted twice in the selection index, the verbal score is the crucial factor in the initial stage of the competition. Students should take this into account in allocating the amount of time they will spend preparing for each section of the PSAT/NMSQT in order to maximize their total score.

Students striving to "win a Merit" will find it advantageous to prepare for the PSAT/NMSQT as they would for the SAT, since the tests are highly similar. Preparing students to take the SAT has become a large industry in itself, and the standardized-exam taker can choose from a wealth of options, including books, courses, computer programs, and coaching sessions that employ every conceivable method—from games theory to massive memorization exercises covering thousands of vocabulary words.

Although only scores from the PSAT/NMSQT taken at the proper time (usually as a junior) can count for the first stage of the National Merit competition, students can take the test in earlier years for practice if their school offers that option. To many students, taking the PSAT/NMSQT as a junior is their first experience in pressure-filled college entrance testing under actual conditions, and this can be a handicap regardless of a student's ability. Taking the PSAT/NMSQT as a sophomore in order to get a taste of the "real thing" is an excellent preparation tool that is often overlooked.

While registering for the PSAT/NMSQT as a sophomore can be a good idea for many students, it is not necessarily recommended for all. The PSAT/NMSQT may involve skills or material (such as topics in algebra and geometry) that students cover in their sophomore-year courses. Without a knowledge of certain subjects, taking the PSAT in the beginning of one's sophomore year can be little more than discouraging for some students. However, a good preparation for all students is to take practice PSATs or SATs on one's own. A sample exam is included in the official PSAT/NMSQT Student Bulletin that is distributed to high schools; also the actual test copies are returned to students with their scores, so a high school sophomore can simply ask an upperclass friend to save a copy. In addition, some SAT prep books (including Peterson's *SAT Success*) offer mock SATs that can serve as useful preparation tools.

When taking a practice test on your own, try to closely simulate the actual testing conditions. Wake yourself up early on the Saturday morning you will take the test and start your practice exam at the time the test is administered at the local high school. Use a timer or stopwatch, and make sure you are not disturbed by phone calls, younger brothers, or any other distractions.

Program Deadlines

The PSAT/NMSQT is administered in late October at high schools throughout the nation. Students must register in advance and pay a small fee (which may be waived in the case of financial hardship). Participants receive their scores through their schools in December. Leading scorers are notified in April, and Letters of Commendation are sent to high school principals in the fall of the student's senior year. Semifinalists are notified through their high schools in September of their senior year.

For Additional Information

Write to: National Merit Scholarship Corporation
One American Plaza
Evanston, Illinois 60201

For information specifically relating to the PSAT/NMSQT, write to:
PSAT/NMSQT
Box 589
Princeton, NJ 08541

National Science Teachers Association/*Discover* Science Scholarship Program

Focus: Science

Who May Enter: Students in 12th grade

Entry Requirement: Essay

Awards: (1) $5000, (3) $1000 scholarships

Sponsor/Administrator: *Discover* magazine/National Science Teachers Association

The National Science Teachers Association (NSTA)/*Discover* Science Scholarship Program is a writing competition for high school seniors. The contest presents a unique challenge: students must write an essay that focuses on an unsolved scientific problem and propose one or more avenues of research as a possible solution. Contestants who can tackle this difficult task have a chance to win substantial scholarship grants and gain national distinction for their efforts.

The scholarship program, which began in 1982, is sponsored by *Discover* magazine, a leading science periodical with a monthly circulation exceeding 850,000. NSTA, an organization of some 20,000 science educators at the primary, secondary, and college levels, is responsible for administering the program. The recognition that contest winners receive from these organizations is further enhanced by the fact that winning entries are sometimes written up in *Discover*.

The first-place national winner receives a $5000 scholarship and a trip to the National Science Teachers Association annual convention. Three runners-up receive scholarships of $1000 each, and honorable mention certificates are presented to six other students. All scholarships are paid directly to the college or university that the recipient will attend.

Rules and Procedures

Students in twelfth grade are eligible to enter the competition. Contestants must prepare an article, not to exceed ten pages (though additional material may appear in appendices), on a specific topic or theme. The student's article must: (1) state what he or she considers to be a major, unsolved problem in science; (2) provide historical perspective concerning the problem, including a summary and critical analysis of relevant scientific work; (3) describe the current status of the problem and justify its importance; and (4) propose an original approach to resolving the problem.

One of the student's current or former science teachers must serve as an adviser and must attest to the validity of the entry. In addition, contestants may seek the advice of a university scientist, medical scientist, or engineer in preparing the article.

Each article must be accompanied by a bibliography and an official entry form, completed and signed by the student and the student's teacher/adviser.

All entries in the NSTA/*Discover* Science program must be original work prepared specifically for the program. If the paper was prepared or submitted in connection with any other program, activity, or publishing project, then the paper is ineligible for consideration. Furthermore, articles submitted in the competition must be the original typed copy of the material. (If the submission appears to be a carbon copy or photocopy, it will be returned to the student and not entered in the contest.)

Contest entries are initially evaluated by a panel consisting of scientists, teachers, and science writers. Criteria on which papers are judged include the following:

- A demonstrated understanding of scientific principles, theories, and laws.

- A clearly stated rationale and adequate documentation to support the scientific problem under discussion.

- The use of clear and simple language that a lay reader can understand.

Ten semifinalists are selected from the pool of entries. Semifinalist entries are sent to *Discover* magazine, where the winning article and three runners-up are selected by a panel of *Discover* writers and editors. Information about the entrant's identity and school is withheld throughout the judging to ensure objectivity in the selection of winners.

Helpful Hints

The topics of the four award-winning articles in the 1982–83 NSTA/ *Discover* competition may offer some insights into the type of specific theme that successful entrants have chosen. Jack Tsao, a graduate of Penn Hills Senior High School in Pittsburgh, now attending Harvard University, won first place and a $5000 scholarship with an essay titled "The Physicists' Search for the Elusive Magnetic Monopole." His paper concerned a subatomic particle with a single magnetic pole, which is a central issue in theoretical physics. The runners-up and winners of $1000 scholarships were Eric Beattie of Hillsborough, California, for an article titled "Spinal Cord Injury and the Regenerative Processes of the Central Nervous System," David Graser of Anchorage, Alaska, for an essay titled "Gravitational Waves," and Christopher Pearl of Bowie, Maryland, for an essay titled "Rain, Rain, Go Away," on the subject of acid rain.

Program Deadlines

Entry materials must be submitted no later than December 1. NSTA notifies all entrants of the program results by February 15.

For Additional Information/Application Forms

Write to: NSTA/*Discover* Science Scholarship Program
National Science Teachers Association
1742 Connecticut Avenue, N.W.
Washington, D.C. 20009

National Society, Daughters of the American Revolution—American History Scholarship Award

Focus:	History
Who May Enter:	Students in 12th grade planning to major in American history; U.S. citizens only
Entry Requirements:	SAT/ACT, essay, recommendations, transcript
Awards:	(1) $8000 scholarship
Deadline:	February 1
Sponsor/Administrator:	National Society, Daughters of the American Revolution

The National Society of the Daughters of the American Revolution (NSDAR), an organization of women descendants of Revolutionary War patriots, conducts various educational and historical activities. Each year the NSDAR awards an $8000 four-year scholarship ($2000 per academic year) to a student in the twelfth grade who is planning to pursue a college education with a major in American history.

Rules and Procedures

To be eligible for the scholarship, an applicant must be a U.S. citizen and a graduating high school senior who ranks in the top third of the class and who plans to major in American history while in college. Applicants must complete a comprehensive application form and prepare an essay (not to exceed 500 words in length) concerning reasons for studying American history. They must also submit three recommendations from high school personnel (principal, guidance counselor, and history teacher), two character references, their high school transcript, and SAT and/or ACT scores.

Program Deadlines

Materials must be submitted to the State Chairman of the DAR Scholarship Committee by February 1.

For More Information/Application Forms

Write to: Office of the Committees
NSDAR
1776 D Street, N.W.
Washington, D.C. 20006

National Society, Daughters of the American Revolution—Caroline E. Holt Educational Fund

Focus:	Nursing
Who May Enter:	Students in 12th grade and high school graduates planning careers in nursing
Entry Requirements:	Recommendations, transcript
Awards:	$300–$500 scholarships (number varies)
Deadline:	April 1
Sponsor/Administrator:	National Society, Daughters of the American Revolution

The National Society of the Daughters of the American Revolution (NSDAR), an organization of women descendants of Revolutionary War patriots, conducts various educational and historical activities. The NSDAR-sponsored Caroline E. Holt Educational Fund provides scholarship grants to individuals for nursing study in amounts ranging from $300 to $500. The number of grants awarded each year varies but in recent years has usually numbered about eight to ten.

Rules and Procedures

High school seniors as well as high school graduates who plan to pursue careers in nursing are eligible to apply for the scholarships. An application must be submitted along with a transcript of grades, a statement of the applicant's financial need, and a brief biographical sketch.

Program Deadlines

Applications must be submitted no later than April 1.

For More Information/Application Forms

Write to: Office of the Committees
NSDAR
1776 D Street, N.W.
Washington, D.C. 20006

National Society of Professional Engineers— Engineering Scholarships

Focus:	Engineering
Who May Enter:	Students in 12th grade planning to study engineering; U.S. citizens and permanent residents only
Entry Requirements:	Class rank, GPA, SAT, application, essay, interview
Awards:	(150 +) $1000 full-tuition scholarships
Deadline:	November 15
Sponsor/Administrator:	NSPE Educational Foundation

The Educational Foundation of the National Society of Professional Engineers (NSPE) offers extensive scholarship opportunities for high school seniors who plan to study engineering. In addition to more than 120 restricted scholarships—which generally are limited to use at a specified college or university or for study in a particular area of specialization—the Foundation offers close to forty unrestricted grants, based strictly on scholarship and academic achievement, that can be used for study in any engineering curriculum accredited by the Accreditation Board for Engineering and Technology. These unrestricted awards include twenty-four regional scholarships ($2000 each), awarded to four winners in each of NSPE's six administrative regions. Among unrestricted grants awarded to individuals with special qualifications, three special scholarships are given to women (two $1000 grants and one renewable 4-year grant of $1000 per year), and three awards of $2000 each are offered to members of minority groups.

Restricted grants may be used for specialized study in such fields as chemical, construction, or petroleum engineering, or for study at such institutions as Boston University, Carnegie-Mellon, Case Western Reserve, Cornell, GMI Engineering and Management Institute, Illinois Institute of Technology, Johns Hopkins, Northwestern, Rice, Southern Methodist University, and Stevens Institute of Technology.

Rules and Procedures

To be eligible for scholarship consideration, applicants must meet the following requirements: (1) be a graduating high school senior planning to study engineering in college, and rank in the top quarter of the class or otherwise be recommended by the high school principal; (2) maintain at least a 3.0 grade-point average (as computed on a 4.0 scale) during the tenth and eleventh grades in high school; (3) score at least 500 on the verbal portion and at least 600 on the math portion of the SAT; and (4) be a U.S. citizen or permanent resident.

Candidates must submit a comprehensive application form and an essay and must be interviewed by a scholarship committee member at a local NSPE chapter. The essay must be one typewritten page (approximately 250 words) long. NSPE describes the four topics on which a student may choose to write the essay:

- Great Engineering Achievement—essay should discuss a major achievement in engineering that has occurred during the last 50 years.

- Conserving Energy Resources—essay should discuss the specific ways an engineer can approach the problem of conserving our limited energy resources.

- My Interest in Engineering—essay should define engineering and explain how you, the applicant, became interested in engineering. You should also discuss the specific field of engineering you are interested in and explain why you wish to enter the practice of engineering.

- Engineering Challenges—essay should discuss specific problems that are most challenging to the applicant as a future engineer and review how the solutions to these problems would best benefit society.

The following scoring is used by the NSPE Education Foundation as the basis for selecting scholarship recipients:

	Maximum points awarded
SAT Math Test Score above minimum requirement	30
SAT Verbal Test Score above minimum requirement	20
Grade-Point Average (tenth and eleventh grades only) above minimum requirement	20
High School Activities	20
Essay	10
Total Points (without financial need)	100
Financial Need (if applicable)	10
Total Points (with financial need)	110

Financial need is considered as part of the selection criteria for only a few of the restricted scholarship awards.

Program Deadlines

Applications must be submitted by November 15.

For Additional Information/Application Forms

Write to: NSPE Educational Foundation
2029 K Street, N.W.
Washington, D.C. 20006

National Society, Sons of the American Revolution— Douglass G. High Historical Oration Contest

Focus:	Public speaking
Who May Enter:	Students in 10th-12th grades
Entry Requirement:	Prepared oration
Awards:	National: (1) $600, (1) $400, (1) $200 cash award; $35 cash awards (number varies) State, local: cash awards (amounts vary); medals
Deadline:	Spring
Sponsor/Administrator:	National Society, Sons of the American Revolution

The Douglass G. High Historical Oration Contest, sponsored by the National Society of the Sons of the American Revolution (SAR), is a competitive public speaking event held on the local, state, and national levels. Students compete by presenting, from memory, an original 5- to 6-minute oration on a subject that deals with the history of the American Revolutionary War and concerns a personality, an event, or a document in that war and its relationship to the nation today. The SAR states as the purpose of the contest:

1. To bring American history to the high school student and focus on events of today.
2. To draw an intelligent relationship between past and present.
3. To dramatically demonstrate freedom of opportunity as a basic right of our national heritage.

4. To place a positive emphasis on the plans of our founding fathers.
5. To demonstrate without fault justice under law in a free society.

Approximately half of the state societies of the SAR nationwide participate in the contest by sponsoring oratorical competitions. Winners of contests held by local SAR chapters advance to the state finals, which are held in conjunction with the annual state SAR convention. State sponsoring societies cover expenses for lodging, meals, and transportation for participants in the state contests. State winners become eligible for national competition and receive all-expense-paid trips to the national contest. The top three winners receive $600, $400, and $200, respectively. All other national finalists receive $35 cash awards. Awards on the state and local level include cash prizes, citizenship medals, and certificates.

Rules and Procedures

Students in the tenth through twelfth grades are eligible to enter the competition. Participants must submit written copies of their speeches in advance of the contest. The student's delivery of the speech should be essentially the same as the written text, and notes may not be used. Five criteria are used in the judging, with equal weight placed on each: composition, delivery, logic, significance, and general excellence. The speaker is scored on a scale of one to ten points for each of these criteria. A minor penalty is assessed for going over or under the time allotted for delivery.

Two weeks before the national contest, a copy of the student's speech together with his or her photograph and a biographical sketch must be submitted to the chairman of the National Oration Committee.

Sample Winning Entry

The following oration was written by Ruth Arnett of Chula Vista, California, first-place national winner in the 1983 Douglass G. High Historical Oration Contest.

It has been said that we are destined to repeat what we fail to learn; the American Revolution was the first of Great Britain's miscalculations, which were repeated over and over, in Africa,

India, China, and most recently with their concerted effort to make "Britain Great Again" with the Falkland Islands crisis, which led to the demise of the British Empire. The American Revolution was the product of economics; true, Parliament's bills had the colonists upset, but it was Lord North hoping to save the faltering East India Tea Company—Britain's economic mainstay—and which sought to undermine the American merchant by selling British tea at scandalously low prices, that prompted the American radicals to organize the Boston Tea Party. As a result, Boston harbor was barricaded, and a whole host of repressive acts ensued from the King, which ultimately led to the start of the revolution.

The war could have been avoided, but only a few men in Britain's Parliament saw the fruitlessness of waging war against men who, unlike their counterparts in India and Africa, were educated, and against supplying troops when sea travel was a slow and hazardous venture, and against fighting in 1,800 unfamiliar miles of wilderness coastline. But the notion of British supremacy prevailed, and still does. I quote: "God in His wisdom had created their (meaning nobility) inferiors in Britain; and He doubtless was responsible for the colonists as well."

The war was won; hence the way was open for the eventual triumph of the American states.

I find it ironic that the words freedom, independence, and liberty are synonymous with war, death, destruction. In my mind nothing can justify the loss of human life. Peaceful measures are always available, but man is a creature of limited vision. We have always waged war, and concentrated our most creative energies on devising weapons of doom, and no doubt always will. However, the war was fought and won, and won by sincere men with sincere aims. We achieved our freedom by human sacrifice; we should be grateful; we should take our freedom seriously. We owe those men that much.

Democracy demands more of its subjects than any other form of government. It demands that each man be responsible for preserving our freedoms, and overseeing the democratic process. But increasingly we see our nation shunning responsibility.

Last April I attended a youth conference at Valley Forge; I learned more in that week than in 16 years of reading out of history books. During that stay I visited the infamous winter encampment. I do not believe I have ever felt, experienced, such a flood of emotion as when I stood on those frozen, desolate, wind- and rain-swept hills, shivering in all earnest—properly fed, and wrapped up in numerous sweaters, a hat, coat, gloves—listening to the souls of dead men. Valley Forge is alive with spirits. Such pride, such anger, such remorse, that after 200 years we have learned nothing; we are losing what we had.

Those men that stayed—many deserted—stricken with typhus, dysentery, body lice, scabies, smallpox, starving, ill clothed, 2,500 died—those that battled against the elements, and emerged in the spring ready to fight and win. They cared enough; they believed in the cause; they stayed. Their battle is our battle. Our battle to preserve our union; we are fighting against society's harsh elements—ignorance and apathy. The winter at Valley Forge never ended. It is our job to believe, truly, in America's merits. Our forefathers fought and won. We can too.

Program Deadlines

Entry blanks are available beginning in January. Local contests are held in the early spring, prior to the state SAR conventions. The national contest is held in June.

For Additional Information

Write to: Col. Stewart B. McCarty Jr., USMC (Ret.)
Chairman, Historical Oration Contest
National Society, Sons of the American Revolution
3222 Prince William Drive
Fairfax, Virginia 22031

Optimist International Oratorical Contest

Focus:	Public speaking
Who May Enter:	Students who are under 16 years old (as of 12/31). Open to students in all countries in which Optimist International clubs exist.
Entry Requirement:	Prepared speech
Awards:	State: (2) $1000 scholarships (1 for boys, 1 for girls) Local: scholarships (number and amounts vary)
Deadline:	Winter
Sponsor/Administrator:	Optimist International

Optimist International, an organization of local service clubs, sponsors numerous programs for young people aimed at encouraging an awareness and involvement in civic affairs and good government. Since 1928 it has held the Optimist International Oratorical Contest, in which students compete for scholarship awards by voicing their views on a selected topic relating to civic responsibility in a 4- to 5-minute prepared speech.

The competition begins with programs conducted by local Optimist clubs, with winners advancing first to zone competition (comprising a group of clubs) and then on to the state finals; there is no national contest. Separate competitions are held for boys and girls. Each first-place winner of a state contest receives a $1000 college scholarship grant.

Scholarships in smaller amounts often are awarded to winners in local and zone contests as well.

Each year a different topic is chosen for the oratorical contest. Recent subjects have tended to be broad and open-ended and have included "Serve With Pride" (1983); "You and I and Tomorrow" (1982); and "Our Commitment to Share" (1981). An interesting feature of the program is that it is aimed at younger students. Participants must be under the age of 16 (thus eliminating many high school juniors and most seniors), and there is no minimum age requirement. This makes the Optimist oratorical program an ideal opportunity for high school freshmen and sophomores to gain recognition and scholarships while building their confidence for future competition in public speaking. It is also a good training ground providing students in junior high school and even elementary school with experience in competitive oratorical competition—and the chance to be a winner.

Rules and Procedures

To enter the contest, a student must be under the age of 16 as of December 31 of the contest year. Contestants must complete a brief entry form (signed by a parent or guardian) and return it to an Optimist Club that is sponsoring a local competition. Age verification records must also be submitted with the entry blank. Each contestant entered in a zone or state contest must also submit a typewritten copy of the oration.

Judging in all local, zone, and state contests is conducted according to the following criteria:

	Maximum point score
Personal Qualities	(20)
(Appearance, poise, personality, attitude)	
Material Organization	(30)
(Adherence to subject, theme, value, logic, color)	
Delivery and Presentation	(30)
(Voice, enunciation, pronunciation, gestures, sincerity, and emphasis)	
Overall Effectiveness	(20)
(Appeal, impression, effect)	
	(100)

All scholarships are payable to the institution of higher learning of the recipient's choice, subject to the approval of Optimist International.

Winners must use their scholarship grants within twelve years of the date when they are received.

Program Deadlines

Local, zone, and state contests are held at varying times, usually in late winter and early spring.

For Additional Information/Application Forms

Contact the Optimist Club in your area, or write to:

Optimist International
4494 Lindell Boulevard
St. Louis, Missouri 63108

President's Committee on Employment of the Handicapped—National Journalism Contest

Focus:	Writing
Who May Enter:	Students in 11th-12th grades in participating states. Also open to students in U.S. territories and PR.
Entry Requirement:	Short article
Awards:	National: (1) $2000, (1) $1500, (1) $1250, (1) $1000, (1) $750 scholarship State, local: scholarships and prizes (number and amounts vary)
Deadline:	Varies
Sponsor/Administrator:	President's Committee on Employment of the Handicapped

The President's Committee on Employment of the Handicapped (PCEH) sponsors a national journalism contest that offers students an opportunity to win scholarship awards while gaining a better perspective on the situations of disabled people. Participants must write a short article on a topic relating to the handicapped, with a different theme selected each year. Recent themes have included "Employers or Employees: Disabled People Working" (1984) and "Independence for Disabled People Through Technology" (1983).

The program begins at the local and state levels, with scholarships or other prizes awarded depending on available funding. The first-place state winners receive all-expense-paid trips to Washington, D.C., to attend the PCEH National Conference, where $6500 in scholarships is awarded to five national winners.

Rules and Procedures

Any eleventh or twelfth grade student attending school in participating states, the District of Columbia, U.S. territories, or Puerto Rico is eligible to compete in the contest, including those students at an equivalent educational level in special institutional programs (such as those for handicapped students). In recent years, an average of thirty-five states have participated annually.

Contest entries should be typed (double-spaced) and must not exceed three pages. Students must submit their articles to the Governor's Committee on Employment of the Handicapped or to the organization authorized to operate the contest in their state. As noted above, not all states participate in the program, so students should contact the Governor's Committee (in their state's capital city) before starting work on their entry.

In describing the judging standards for the contest, the President's Committee notes that the use of investigative-reporting techniques will count heavily in the evaluation of entries. Other factors taken into consideration include evidence of the student's initiative in obtaining information through personal interviews and observations and his or her demonstrated familiarity both with programs affecting disabled people and with individual organizations concerned with disability. Articles are also judged on the use of good composition principles, logical organization of the material, and clarity of expression.

Helpful Hints

The literature distributed by the President's Committee offers useful tips to aspiring contestants, including a discussion of the current contest topic and possible ways to approach writing the article. It is important to demonstrate in the article a thorough knowledge of organizations and special programs for the disabled. The information sources listed in the contest literature are valuable sources of research and should not be ignored.

Evidence of the journalistic merit of the article, as demonstrated both in its content and its suitability for publication in local newspapers, is an important factor in the judging. Students are encouraged to consult their journalism or English teachers or reporters and editors on local or school newspapers for help in preparing their entry. If possible, they should enter articles in the contest that have been published in high school or local newspapers. Sending a copy of a published version of the article along with the typed entry is likely to enhance the article's standing in the competition.

Several scholarship winners in the 1983 contest advise that contestants be sure to allow themselves ample time to work on the article. Lee Ann Blackman of Albertville, Alabama, fourth-place national winner, writes, "I would suggest that students begin working on the essay about four months before the deadline." First-place national winner V. Kathleen Reid advises that contestants be certain to seek an adviser (such as an English teacher) to help them with the project, and she further suggests, "Make sure your research is positive and relates directly to the topic."

Sample Winning Entry

Independence for Disabled People Through Technology
by V. Kathleen Reid
(First Place, President's Committee on Employment of the
Handicapped National Journalism Contest, 1983)

He is one of the 24,498 people who attend the University of South Carolina.

He is one of the millions of people who saw *Star Wars* more than once.

He is one of the 5,000 deaf people in South Carolina.

Twenty-seven-year-old Steve Rhodes lost his hearing when he contracted Spinal Meningitis at age five. The disease left him profoundly deaf. His speech is hard for the untrained ear to understand.

Steve's day begins with flashing lights.

"Before he left home, his parents took care of the things he needed to hear, such as an alarm clock, the doorbell, and the telephone," Barbara Porter, Steve's interpreter, said.

When Steve moved to an apartment of his own, he realized he would have to find ways to do the little things his parents had always done. He bought a device that is connected to a timer and light to wake himself up. Steve also had to get similar devices for the doorbell and telephone.

When Steve uses a telephone, he doesn't put a receiver to his ear and speak. He uses a telecommunication device for the deaf (TDD). The TDD has a small screen and a typewriter. Steve types his part of the conversation and receives a typewritten response from the person on the other end.

Steve is looking forward to a new device that is still in the developing stages.

"A company in Atlanta is developing a telephone device which will take what I type and change it to a voice, and then change the voice to printed words," Steve said.

The device will make communication much easier for him because with the TDD he can only "talk" to others who have one.

Steve attended Gallaudet College, the only liberal arts college for the deaf in the world, and the University of Nebraska before moving to South Carolina to work. Steve's parents were willing to allow him to leave home to further his education with the manual language of the deaf.

While working at the R. L. Bryan Printing Company, Steve decided to further his education, so he began to attend the University of South Carolina part-time. Eventually, he quit his job and became a full-time student and is presently in the graduate program.

Steve has a research assistantship. He uses computers to research grain shapes in the ocean to determine the origin of rocks. Steve says that computers have helped him overcome a big barrier in his life.

"The computer has been a wonderful technological advance for me and my work because it has helped break down the communication barrier. Working with a computer doesn't require much communication between me and a hearing person."

For entertainment, Steve does the same things that a hearing person does. He rides a bicycle, reads, and goes to the movies.

"I saw *Star Wars* eight times. I couldn't hear what's being said, but I really enjoy the action," Steve said.

Steve also watches television. He has a device attached to his television that permits him to read the conversation.

"It's nice to be able to watch television and know what is being said, but there are too few captioned programs," Steve said.

Steve says there is one advancement that has helped deaf people more than all the technological ones put together.

"The biggest advance is simply hearing people accepting the deaf as 'normal' people with communication being the only real barrier."

Program Deadlines

Deadlines vary from state to state. State winners are selected and entered in the national competition by March 1.

For Additional Information

Contact the Governor's Committee on Employment of the Handicapped, in your state capital, or write to:

National Journalism Contest—JEC
President's Committee on Employment of the Handicapped
1111 20th Street, N.W., Suite 600
Washington, D.C. 20036

Quill & Scroll Society— Edward J. Nell Memorial Scholarship Program

Focus: Journalism

Who May Enter: Students in 9th-12th grades

Entry Requirements: Writing/photography samples or test on current events. *Advanced level:* essay

Awards: (2) $1000, (8) $500 scholarships

Deadline: Writing/Photography Contest: early February; Current Events Quiz: early March

Sponsor/Administrator: Quill and Scroll

Quill and Scroll, the international honorary society for high school journalists, sponsors two national contests through which eligible students may participate in a scholarship awards program. All high school students are eligible to participate in the National Writing/ Photography Contest and Current Events Quiz; membership in Quill and Scroll is not required. Although these contests do not offer monetary awards, national winners in either competition who plan to major in journalism in college become eligible to compete for the Nell Memorial Scholarships in their senior year. Ten scholarships are generally awarded through this program annually—two awards of $1000 each and eight awards of $500 each.

Rules and Procedures

Any student in the ninth through the twelfth grade is eligible to compete in either the National Writing/Photography Contest or the

Current Events Quiz. The National Writing/Photography Contest judges student work that has been published in a high school or professional newspaper. Awards are made in eight divisions: editorial, editorial cartoon, news story, feature story, investigative reporting, advertisement, sports story, and photography. Each school is limited to two entries per division, and one student may submit any or all of the school's allotted entries. There is a $1 fee for each division entered, up to a maximum charge of $8. The top 5 percent of the entrants in the Writing/Photography Contest are named national winners.

The Current Events Quiz is prepared by the Gallup Poll and contains approximately 100 questions involving current news events. The test is graded on a scale of 100 points. Each school may submit only its highest-scoring entry to the national competition. The top 5–8 percent of the entrants in the contest are named national winners (in recent years, grades of 90–92 percent have been the minimum qualifying scores for national winners).

National winners in either contest who are planning to major in journalism while in college are eligible to apply for an Edward J. Nell Memorial Scholarship. Only seniors may apply for these scholarships; students who are contest winners in either their sophomore or junior year may later apply as seniors.

Those who are eligible should request the scholarship application form early in their senior year. As part of the application, candidates for the Nell Memorial Scholarships must write a letter of not more than 500 words outlining their journalistic experience in high school. Scholarship applicants must sign a statement of intent to major in journalism at a college or university offering such a major.

Scholarship winners are selected from the pool of contest finalists based on the following:

- academic achievement

- potential for journalism career (based on a review of writing samples)

- leadership qualities and potential

- financial need

- communication skills evidenced in the completed application form and associated written statements

Helpful Hints

Writing/Photography Contest—To get an idea of what constitutes a successful writing entry, students should study the articles appearing in

Quill and Scroll magazine. Attending a high school journalism conference (such as the Columbia Scholastic Press Association conference in New York) is another valuable way to gain insights on how to produce quality high school newspaper writing and photography.

Current Events Quiz—The 1983 quiz was organized into four sections. Part I contained 41 multiple-choice questions drawn primarily from the fields of foreign affairs, economics, politics, and domestic issues; additional questions were selected from other areas, including sports and the arts. Part II featured 20 matching problems in which the contestant was required to match the names of individuals with statements about them. Part III consisted of 15 "true or false" questions, and Part IV was composed of 21 matching problems requiring that cities be matched with the corresponding country in which they are located. A good way to prepare for the quiz is to read a major news magazine thoroughly for an extended period and to carefully review the basics of world geography.

Sample Test Questions

The following are sample questions from the 1983 Quill and Scroll Current Events Quiz:

Multiple Choice
1. The reason for the Reagan Administration's boycott of the Soviet natural gas pipeline was to (a) protest the Soviet invasion of Afghanistan (b) retaliate for the Soviet crackdown in Poland (c) put pressure on the Soviets to ban production of nuclear weapons (d) punish the Soviets for aiding Argentina in the Falklands Island war. (answer: b)
2. Last October, _____ reached a post–World War II high of 10.4% in the U.S. (a) inflation (b) crime (c) trading on the stock exchange (d) unemployment (answer: d)
3. Considered one of the most stable countries in Africa, _____ 19-year background of political stability was interrupted when its air force unsuccessfully attempted to overthrow the government. (a) Kenya's (b) Gabon's (c) Botswana's (d) Algeria's (answer: a)
4. Which group entered the Shatila Sabra camps in Beirut and massacred Palestinian refugees? (a) Christian Phalangists (b) PLO

army (c) Israeli army (d) Syrian army (answer: a)
5. Budget Director David Stockman was reprimanded by President Reagan for calling the President's economic policy (a) "voodoo economics" (b) "a bailout for the rich" (c) "a slogan, not really a theory" (d) "a failure." (answer: b)
6. The boxing event of 1982 pitted _____ against reigning champion _____ in a battle for the heavyweight title.
(a) Gerry Cooney, George Foreman (b) Earnie Shavers, Larry Holmes (c) Gerry Cooney, Larry Holmes (d) Earnie Shavers, George Foreman (answer: c)
7. The biography of a world leader was published by Marvel Comics. Who is he/she? (a) Pope John Paul II (b) Margaret Thatcher (c) Menachem Begin (d) Ronald Reagan (answer: a)

True or False
1. A constitutional amendment requiring a balanced federal budget was passed by Congress. (false)
2. The St. Louis Cardinals won the 1982 baseball World Series. (true)
3. Elections resulted in the Spanish Socialist Workers' Party gaining control of the Spanish government. (true)
4. President Reagan was part of the United States official delegation attending Leonid Brezhnev's funeral. (false)

Program Deadlines
The deadline for submissions to the Writing/Photography Contest is early February. Eligible seniors should request application forms for the Nell Scholarships in September or October.

For Additional Information
Write to: Quill and Scroll Society
School of Journalism and Mass Communication
The University of Iowa
Iowa City, Iowa 52242

Scholastic Art Awards

Focus:	Art
Who May Enter:	Students in 7th-12th grades. Also open to students in U.S. territories and to those attending U.S.-sponsored schools abroad.
Entry Requirements:	Portfolio, application, recommendation, transcript
Awards:	(About 100) full-tuition scholarships; cash awards (number and amounts vary)
Deadline:	Varies
Sponsor/Administrator:	Scholastic, Inc.

In conjunction with such major corporations as Kodak, Smith-Corona, NBC, and Hallmark Cards, Scholastic conducts competitions in three areas—art, photography, and writing—that attract an estimated 200,000 entrants each year. In addition to national recognition, students compete for cash prizes and scholarship awards.

The Scholastic Art Awards program offers a variety of rewards for talented student artists. In addition to honorary keys and medals, cash awards, and the chance to see one's work shown in a national exhibition, the competition provides high school seniors with the opportunity to win one-year full-tuition art scholarships offered by colleges and universities across the nation. The art program features an annual National High School Art Exhibition, which in past years has been held at the Corcoran Gallery and School of Art in Washington, D.C., and at the Parsons School of Design and Union Carbide Building in New York City, among other prestigious sites.

Students may enter work in any of fourteen categories of competition: acrylics; graphic design; ink drawing; jewelry; mixed media; oil painting; pastels, crayon, or charcoal; pencil drawing; pottery; printmaking; sculpture; textile design; two- and three-dimensional design; and watercolor.

The top-ranking entrants in regional competition are awarded gold achievement keys and certificates of merit. In addition, cash awards of $100 are presented for the best painting or drawing from each sponsored region. From the pool of key-winning entries a group of blue-ribbon regional finalists is selected, with the number of winners proportional to the population of the region. This group then advances to national competition.

Engraved gold medals are presented to more than 300 national winners in the 14 categories of competition. Three cash awards of $1000 each and two cash awards of $500 each are also given for outstanding portfolios entered in the national competition. In addition, close to 100 full-tuition scholarships to art schools are offered to top contestants who are high school seniors.

Rules and Procedures

The program is open to all students in seventh through twelfth grades. Separate competitions are conducted for students in two groups: Group I (grades 7-9) and Group II (grades 10-12).

Each portfolio of artwork must be accompanied by an official entry blank, signed by a teacher who is familiar with the student's work and able to attest to its originality. Specific instructions for packing and shipping entries are included in the contest rules booklet.

In sponsored regions, the portfolio must be submitted to the regional sponsor. The regional jury will judge each work within the portfolio for individual honors and will also select the portfolios that are to advance to the national competition. A selected number of entries from schools in unsponsored areas are also accepted for national judging. These entries are screened by a preliminary jury, with the best work then judged along with the regional finalists.

Only graduating high school seniors may apply for the college scholarships. Eligible students must submit a portfolio of eight examples of their best work, including at least three drawings. Applicants must also submit a scholarship application form together with the high school transcript and a confidential personal rating form filled out by the student's teacher or principal. The national scholarship jury consists of artists and educators who are associated with leading art schools and universities nationwide.

Although some sixty art schools and colleges offer scholarships through the Scholastic Art Awards program, candidates are required to list three preferred schools when applying for the awards. Students should request catalogs from the schools they expect to list as preferences well in advance of the competition in order to acquaint themselves with courses and requirements. Applicants must be able to meet the entrance requirements of the schools they list to be eligible to receive a scholarship.

Helpful Hints

The contest rules booklet offers this advice to seniors who plan to enter the scholarship competition: "Applicants should be in at least the academic upper half of the graduating class. Most art schools expect candidates to have good grades in all subjects."

These observations are also offered to students: "Many colleges will make available the scholarship only if you have previously applied for admission and been accepted. More and more institutions are requiring evidence of financial need for scholarship aid. Often they will expect that a Financial Aid Form (FAF) will have been filed with the College Scholarship Service."

Contestants should carefully review the submissions of national winners in Scholastic programs of previous years to gain insights into the techniques, styles, and approaches of successful entrants. Published collections of award-winning entries from previous contests may be ordered directly from Scholastic Book Service, P.O. Box 7502, 2931 East McCarty Street, Jefferson City, Missouri 65102. *Grab Me a Bus* ($1.75) and *Mad Sad and Glad* ($1.95) contain sample art award winners.

Program Deadlines

Rules books are available October 1. Deadlines for regional contests vary. Entries submitted from schools not located in a sponsored region must be received by Scholastic in New York during the first two weeks in February. Portfolios and other entries are returned to the schools by late April or early May. Winners of national honors are notified in May.

For Additional Information/Application Forms

Write to: Scholastic Art Awards
Scholastic, Inc.
730 Broadway
New York, New York 10003

Scholastic Photography Awards

Focus: Photography

Who May Enter: Students in 7th-12th grades. Also open to students in U.S. territories and those attending U.S.-sponsored schools abroad.

Entry Requirements: Photography portfolio, application, recommendations, transcript

Awards: (1) $4000, (1) $2000, (1) $1000, (1) $500 scholarship; (up to 250) cash awards in amounts of $100, $50, $25 each

Deadline: February

Sponsor/Administrator: Eastman Kodak Company/Scholastic, Inc.

In conjunction with such major corporations as Kodak, Smith-Corona, NBC, and Hallmark Cards, Scholastic conducts competitions in three areas—art, photography, and writing—that attract an estimated 200,000 entrants each year. In addition to national recognition, students compete for cash prizes and scholarship awards.

For the student with a serious interest in photography, the Scholastic Photography Awards program, sponsored by the Eastman Kodak Company, offers an outstanding opportunity to receive national recognition, cash prizes, and scholarships. Photos qualifying for national honors are exhibited in the Scholastic/Kodak Photography Awards National Exhibition in New York City. Selected prize-winning prints receive further recognition through a traveling exhibit, prepared by Kodak, which tours U.S. schools, libraries, and hospitals. The cash prizes are numerous on the national level, and students win preliminary honors in regional Scholastic Art exhibitions (sixty were conducted in 1982).

A special opportunity is available to contestants who are college-bound seniors: four scholarship grants worth $2000, $1000, $500, and $250, respectively, are awarded on the basis of portfolios of 10 prints; awards of $100 each are given for 15 portfolios receiving honorable mention. In all, contestants can win up to 250 cash awards (in amounts of $100, $50, and $20) which together total $9500. Regional awards include medallions of excellence, gold achievement keys, and certificates of merit.

Rules and Procedures

High school and junior high school students are eligible to enter the program. Two separate competitions are held for students according to grade level—Group I for grades 7–9 and Group II for grades 10–12. Group I entrants may compete in two classifications: black-and-white or color. Group II students may compete for awards in four categories: black-and-white, color, black-and-white experimental, and color experimental.

Students wishing to enter the contest should first check to see if their school is in an area where a regional exhibition will be held (this information is listed in the official rules booklet). If the student's school is within the listed regions, entries and portfolios must be submitted to the regional sponsors for preliminary judging at the times indicated. Contestants whose schools do not have a regional sponsor should send entries directly to Scholastic, Inc., in New York. Their entries come before a preliminary jury, which selects the work that will later be judged for national honors along with the regional finalists.

Gold achievement keys are awarded by regional sponsors to outstanding entries in each region administered by the program. From the key-winning photos the judges select blue-ribbon finalists. The number of finalists in each region is proportional to the region's population. Regional sponsors forward the finalist entries to the national headquarters of Scholastic, Inc., to be judged for national awards. A special medallion is given for the best photograph in each sponsored region.

To compete for the scholarship grants, contestants must be graduating seniors. Applicants must submit one portfolio containing ten prints; transparencies are not acceptable, and the portfolio should include a minimum of five black-and-white prints. Scholarship candidates must also submit a scholarship application, a recommendation form filled out by a teacher, and the high school transcript. After the scholarship judging is completed, selected entries, other than portfolio winners, are awarded cash prizes.

When entering photos in the contest, students should be sure to submit the names and addresses of any recognizable people who appear in their work. Written consent of the people photographed will be required before a national prize can be awarded.

Helpful Hints

Contestants can gain insights into the different techniques and styles of winners in the Scholastic Photography Awards program by attending the national exhibition in New York City, by visiting one of the regional Scholastic art exhibitions, or by viewing the winning photos on the national tour. Locations and times of regional exhibitions can be obtained by contacting the regional sponsors or the national office of Scholastic, Inc.

Contestants should carefully review the submissions of national winners in Scholastic programs of previous years to gain insights into the techniques, styles, and approaches of successful entrants. Published collections of award-winning entries from previous contests may be ordered directly from Scholastic Book Service, P.O. Box 7502, 2931 East McCarty Street, Jefferson City, Missouri 65102. *Grab Me a Bus* ($1.75) and *Mad Sad and Glad* ($1.95) contain samples of award-winning photographs.

Program Deadlines

Rules books and scholarship applications are available October 1. Deadlines for submissions to most regional contests are in January. Entries from schools without regional sponsors must be received at the Scholastic offices in New York during the first two weeks in February. Entries not winning national awards are returned to the entrant's teacher in late March. Winners of national honors are notified through their high school or junior high school principal in early May.

For Additional Information/Application Forms

Write to: Scholastic Photography Awards
            Scholastic, Inc.
            730 Broadway
            New York, New York 10003

Scholastic Writing Awards

Focus: Writing

Who May Enter: Students in 7th-12th grades who are under 20 years old. Also open to students in U.S. territories and those attending U.S.-sponsored schools abroad.

Entry Requirements: Writing submissions: short stories/poetry/essays/humor

Awards: (2) $1500, (4) $1000, (3) $250 scholarships; (2) $1500 cash awards; numerous $10–$250 cash awards

Deadline: January

Sponsor/Administrator: Scholastic, Inc.

In conjunction with such major corporations as Kodak, Smith-Corona, NBC, and Hallmark Cards, Scholastic conducts competitions in three areas—art, photography, and writing—that attract an estimated 200,000 entrants each year. In addition to national recognition, students compete for cash prizes and scholarship awards.

The Scholastic Writing Awards competition provides aspiring student writers with an opportunity to achieve many of their highest goals—national recognition, scholarships, and publication—in a single competition. Student writing submitted to the contest is judged and evaluated by distinguished authors, editors, and educators. All entrants compete for cash awards; high school seniors are eligible for college scholarship grants as well. Award-winning manuscripts may be selected for inclusion in such Scholastic publications as *Literary Cavalcade, Junior Scholastic, Scholastic Voice,* and *Scholastic Scope.*

Nancy Hanks Memorial Awards of $1500 each are presented to two seniors who demonstrate outstanding writing ability and high academic standing. Tuition scholarships of $1000 are also awarded to seniors submitting the most outstanding work in each of four categories: short story, poetry, critical review, and dramatic script. Two tuition grants of $250 each are given to seniors selected for their general creative writing ability, and a special award of $250 is given to a senior showing outstanding ability in several classifications of competition. In addition, up to thirty cash prizes are offered in each classification in amounts ranging from $10 to $250. Portable electric typewriters are awarded for up to seven outstanding entries in the Short Story and Short-Short Story classifications.

Rules and Procedures

Students in the seventh through twelfth grades may compete in the program, which is organized into two divisions: the Senior Division (grades 10–12) and the Junior Division (grades 7–9). Entries may be submitted in the following classifications:

Senior Division

- *Short Story*—A short fictional narrative about one or more characters living through a single significant action or experience. Length: 1,300 to 3,000 words.

- *Short-Short Story*—A very tightly constructed story that concentrates on one central idea, conflict, or situation. Length: 600 to 1,300 words.

- *Poetry*—One poem or a group of poems (not necessarily related in subject) in any form of verse, rhymed or free. Length: at least 50 lines and not more than 200 lines. (Poetry awards are given for the entire entry, not for any part thereof.)

- *Critical Review*—An evaluation or critical account of a work of literature (novel, short story, essay, play, or poem) by a particular author. The review should express ideas and opinions as well as reflect an understanding of the medium that is being considered. Length: 600 to 1,200 words.

- *Essay*—Either of the following: (1) a personal essay—a highly personal piece of nonfiction intended to instruct, explain, or entertain; (2) a formal essay—a newspaper editorial or serious piece of nonfiction intended to convey information or to maintain and defend a point of view. Length: 600 to 1,500 words.

- *Humor*—A satire, parody, or original humorous anecdote in short story or article form. Length: 600 to 1,500 words.

- *Dramatic Script*—an original radio, television, or film script, or a one-act play for the stage. Adaptations of stories, novels, or plays by other writers are not acceptable. Length: not to exceed 30 minutes of performing time.

Junior Division

- *Essay*—A piece of nonfiction on any interesting topic—a personal experience, an event, or a national or world problem. It may be serious or humorous, but it should reflect the writer's own thoughts and feelings about the subject. Length: 500 to 1,500 words.

- *Poetry*—A poem or a group of poems (not necessarily related in subject) in any form of verse, rhymed or free. Length: at least 35 lines and not more than 100 lines. (An award in this classification is given for the entire entry, not for any part thereof.)

- *Short Story*—A short narrative about actual or imaginary characters and what happened to them. Length: 600 to 1,800 words.

Each entry must be submitted with an official entry blank. Students may submit entries independently or through their teacher. If the entry is submitted independently, it must be signed by a teacher in the student's school to confirm the originality of the writing. Joint authorship is not permitted.

A student may enter up to three different pieces of writing in each classification, except poetry, where only one entry from each student is acceptable. Students are also permitted to submit entries in several different classifications. However, no manuscript may be submitted in more than one category; for example, a humorous short story cannot be submitted in both the Humor and Short Story categories.

Entries are judged initially by creative writing teachers who are affiliated with the National Writing Project. Entries placed in the finalists category are then sent for final evaluation to a team of judges from the literary community. Final judges in the 1982 Scholastic Writing

Awards included Jerzy Kozinski (author of *Being There*) and best-selling humorist Erma Bombeck.

Helpful Hints

Before the 1982 contest, Scholastic, Inc., distributed a pamphlet to teachers offering insights for helping students prepare successful entries. The booklet offered these observations: "Often the danger for young writers is their wish to make overly ambitious statements about big themes: love, war, God, death. You might suggest that most stories of depth and sensitivity are written on a small scale: one character's experience of a relationship, one family's reaction to a death, one child's sense of security in a confusing world. This is an area in which literary study can be useful in conjunction with writing practice; by seeing how other writers have approached the grand themes through concentration on just a few incidents, characters, and descriptions, students may learn to set more practical limits to their own subjects."

Students are encouraged to ask their teachers for help and guidance in writing their entries. This might include general constructive criticism and suggestions as well as specific review of the finished work for errors in spelling, punctuation, or grammar.

Contestants should carefully review the submissions of national winners in Scholastic programs of previous years to gain insights into the techniques, styles, and approaches of successful entrants. Published collections of award-winning entries from previous contests may be ordered directly from Scholastic Book Service, P.O. Box 7502, 2931 East McCarty Street, Jefferson City, Missouri 65102. *Grab Me a Bus* ($1.75), *Mad Sad and Glad* ($1.95), and *Shadows in the Light* ($1.50) contain award-winning writing samples.

Program Deadlines

The deadline for entries is usually the last week in January. Students should submit their work directly to Scholastic, Inc., except if they live in one of the regions listed below. In these areas, regional sponsors participate in the initial judging of student entries.

Regional Sponsors

Central Pennsylvania area (Adams, Cumberland, Dauphin, Lebanon, Lycoming, Perry, and York counties as well as Lancaster County) — deadline: mid-December.

Greater Houston area (Brazoria, Chambers, Fort Bend, Galveston, Harris, Liberty, Montgomery, and Waller counties) —deadline: early January.

For Additional Information/Application Forms

Write to: Scholastic Writing Awards
Scholastic, Inc.
730 Broadway
New York, New York 10003

The Scripps-Howard Foundation Scholarships

Focus: Journalism

Who May Enter: Students planning full-time undergraduate or graduate study to prepare for a career in the news media; U.S. citizens or U.S. visa holders only

Entry Requirements: Journalism-related experience, GPA, recommendations, need

Awards: Scholarships of up to $2000/yr (number varies)

Deadline: December 20

Sponsor/Administrator: The Scripps-Howard Foundation

The Scripps-Howard Foundation conducts an annual national competition for scholarship candidates in accordance with its mission to improve the quality of journalism. Scholarships are awarded for the use of students who plan to pursue (or are currently engaged in) full-time undergraduate or graduate study at a college or university in preparation for a career in the news media. The term *news media* here embraces print and broadcast journalism, including both editorial and business operations of newspapers, news magazines, radio, or television. Preference is given to college juniors and seniors and graduate students; to previous recipients; and to students residing in, or attending a college or university located in, communities served by Scripps-Howard properties.

Scholarships range up to a maximum of $2000 per academic year. They are not automatically renewed; recipients must reapply annually. The number of scholarships varies, and the awards are highly competitive. For the academic year 1983–84, of 1,400 applications submitted, 241 students were awarded scholarships.

Rules and Procedures

Scholarship applicants must fulfill the following eligibility requirements:

- Submit evidence of some kind of journalism-related work experience, which may include working for a high school or college newspaper, magazine, or radio or TV station or for an employer in the news media industry. One or more letters of recommendation are required from the faculty member responsible for the publication or station or from the outside employer.

- Attain a grade-point average of at least 3.5 of possible 4.

- Demonstrate financial need as determined by the College Scholarship Service of the College Board. Applicants must work to pay part of their educational expenses.

- Hold U.S. citizenship or have a valid U.S. visa.

- Choose a school offering a strong curriculum in a journalism-related field.

Program Deadline

Students interested in applying for the awards should send a typed, self-addressed mailing label marked "Scholarship Application" to the Scripps-Howard Foundation by December 20. Scholarship application packets are sent to students in early January and must be returned to the Foundation by February 15. All applicants are notified by May 15.

For Application Forms

Write to: The Scripps-Howard Foundation
1100 Central Trust Tower
Cincinnati, Ohio 45202

Society of Women Engineers Scholarship Program

Focus:	Engineering
Who May Enter:	High school girls accepted into an engineering curriculum (GE awards open to U.S. citizens or permanent residents only)
Entry Requirements:	Application, GPA, PSAT, SAT/ACT, ACH, work experience, recommendations, essay
Awards:	(3) $1000/yr renewable General Electric Scholarships (3) $1000 Westinghouse Scholarships
Deadline:	July 1
Sponsors/Administrator:	General Electric, Westinghouse/Society of Women Engineers

The Society of Women Engineers (SWE) is a nonprofit educational service organization of graduate engineers dedicated to encouraging women engineers to attain high levels of educational and professional achievement. The organization administers two scholarship funds for women students who are entering their freshman year of college and plan to study engineering. The General Electric Foundation Scholarships are $1000 grants awarded each year to three outstanding women students. They are renewable for up to three years with continued academic achievement. The $1000 Westinghouse Scholarships (also awarded to three outstanding women candidates) were established in honor of Bertha Lamme, one of the first women to receive a degree in engineering in the United States (1893) and the first woman engineer employed by Westinghouse. Both scholarship funds are aimed at providing a source of financial support for talented women striving to succeed in a traditionally male-dominated field.

Rules and Procedures

The scholarships are open to women who have been accepted for enrollment at an accredited college or university and plan to major in engineering. Applicants must be U.S. citizens or permanent residents to be eligible for the General Electric scholarships.

All applicants are automatically considered for both the General Electric and Westinghouse scholarships. Scholarship candidates must complete an application form listing high school grade-point average, class rank, national test scores (PSAT, SAT/ACT, ACH), activities, honors, hobbies, and work experience. Two letters of reference are required, one from a high school teacher and one from a person not related to the applicant who has known her for two or more years. Students must submit an official copy of their high school transcript and a letter or statement from an accredited college or university indicating acceptance into an undergraduate engineering curriculum for the next academic year. Each applicant must write a statement, not more than 500 words in length, telling why she would like to be an engineer and why she is seeking a scholarship. Although not required to do so, scholarship candidates may provide financial information such as sources of income and anticipated college expenses. Students should include this information on the application form only if they wish financial need to be taken into consideration when the application is reviewed.

Program Deadlines

Application forms are available from March through June. All materials must be submitted by July 1. Scholarship recipients are notified by the middle of September.

For Additional Information/Application Forms

Write to: Society of Women Engineers
United Engineering Center, Room 305
345 East 47th Street
New York, NY 10017

Soroptimist Foundation Youth Citizenship Awards

Focus:	Leadership, citizenship, community service
Who May Enter:	Students in 12th grade who are under 21 years old (as of 6/1)
Entry Requirements:	Application, essays, recommendations
Awards:	National: (1) $2000 cash award Regional: (23) $1250 cash awards Local: varying cash awards
Deadline:	December 15
Sponsor/Administrator:	Soroptimist Foundation

The Soroptimist Foundation offers regional Youth Citizenship Awards "to recognize outstanding contributions by young people to improve the quality of life of their fellow citizens in their schools, communities, country, and world." The Foundation is part of Soroptimist International of the Americas, which is a branch of Soroptimist International, a worldwide service organization for professional and executive business women. The awards program is a unique opportunity for students of both sexes who have played an active and leading role in their schools and communities. The competition is based solely on factors such as service and leadership; high school grades, SAT scores, grade-point average, and class rank are not specifically considered. Students who have excelled outside the classroom are thus competitive candidates for these awards.

A total of twenty-three $1250 cash awards are given annually—one to each winner within the twenty-three designated regions of Soroptimist International of the Americas. One student from among the regional winners is named the national finalist and receives an additional $2000. Some local Soroptimist clubs give individual awards of varying amounts. All awards are cash grants to be used by the recipients in a manner that will further their career goals.

Rules and Procedures

To be eligible for the scholarships, applicants must be high school seniors and under 21 years of age as of June 1 of the current academic year. Awards candidates must complete a four-page application in which they describe career plans and goals, school activities, community activities, and activities beyond the community. Applicants must also write three short essays (not to exceed 125 words each) on the following topics:

- Briefly describe your family responsibilities.

- What do you consider your citizenship responsibility in the community?

- How do you view your role as a citizen of the world?

In addition, candidates must submit letters of recommendation from three adults not related to the applicant who are familiar with three different areas of the student's activities (e.g., a teacher, community leader, and clergyman).

The contest literature lists four criteria by which applicants are evaluated:

- *Service*—Applicant must have taken an active part in service in the home, school, and community, with evidence of cooperation, courtesy, and consideration for others.

- *Dependability*—Applicant must have executed responsibilities with honesty, loyalty, and reliability.

- *Leadership*—Applicant must have demonstrated ability to lead with self-control, dignity, and responsibility.

- *Clear sense of purpose*—Applicant must have pursued selected endeavors with sincerity and integrity.

Helpful Hints

In a review of the credentials of recent regional award winners, several common qualifications emerge. Most of the winners had been involved in some sort of volunteer work—hospital work and work with the mentally retarded, with the aged, with the disabled or disadvantaged, or for the March of Dimes and similar organizations were common among the award recipients. Many were also involved in church groups. In the area of school activities, the award winners tended to be well rounded, with sports, music, student government, and school publications being typical interests.

The following description of Robin Florzak, a Midwestern regional winner and recipient of the national finalist award in 1981, appeared in the magazine of Soroptimist International of the Americas: "An Illinois State Scholar, Robin has earned three varsity letters in track and cross-country in her high school. She is city editor of a youth-oriented news magazine in the Chicago area, with a circulation of nearly 70,000. She has compiled varied experience in audiovisual production, serving as teen producer of a prime-time television program on teenage sexuality for NBC in Chicago, coproduced a video documentary shown on public TV and recently coproduced an award-winning videotape submitted to the Chicago Metro History Fair and the Chicago Public School Video Fair. She also serves as coproducer of her high school radio station. It isn't surprising that her career interest lies in the media, particularly in both the creative and management aspects of print and broadcast journalism."

In completing the application and preparing the essays, entrants should try to distinguish themselves in some unique or creative way. In particular, they should try to demonstrate how their involvement in school and community activities while in high school will be a good preparation for their future career.

An apparent similarity among many past award winners—and an important factor behind their success—is the specific, clearly defined humanitarian career goals they have set for themselves. Career objectives described by past award recipients have included the study of international relations and work with Third World countries; social welfare work, particularly with mentally retarded children; research in genetics with special emphasis on cancer and/or birth defects; and politics and community action. Other frequently cited career choices among award recipients have included medicine and law.

Program Deadlines
Local Soroptimist clubs must receive all completed applications by December 15.

For Additional Information/Application Forms
Write to: The Soroptimist Foundation, Inc.
1616 Walnut Street
Philadelphia, Pennsylvania 19103

That's Incredible Scholarship Award

Focus:	Writing
Who May Enter:	Students in 9th-12th grades
Entry Requirement:	Story proposal
Awards:	(1) $2500 scholarship
Deadline:	October 1
Sponsor/Administrator:	Alan Landsburg Productions

That's Incredible! is a popular prime-time television show featuring unusual or surprising real-life events and stunts that are extraordinary in nature. Its producer sponsors an annual writing contest, in which high school students are invited to prepare and submit a story proposal suitable for the television show. Entries selected as finalists in the competition are considered for telecasting on the program, and the author of the best story proposal receives a $2500 scholarship award.

Rules and Procedures

To be eligible to participate in the contest, students must be registered full- or part-time in a U.S. high school. Up to three submissions from any one high school may be entered in the competition. The story proposals must be typed (double-spaced) and may be up to two pages long.

Program Deadlines

The deadline for submissions is October 1.

For More Information/Application Forms

Write to: Alan Landsburg Productions
             11811 West Olympic Boulevard
             Los Angeles, California 90064

TIME Education Program Student Writing Contest

Focus: Writing/Journalism

Who May Enter: Students in 9th-12th grades

Entry Requirements: Essay/political cartoon

Awards: (3) $5000 scholarships

Deadline: March 1

Sponsor/Administrator: TIME Education Program

The *TIME* Education Program Student Writing Contest is more than a source of scholarship dollars; it presents a compelling challenge to any high school student with an interest in journalism or creative writing. While competing for college money, participants in the *TIME* writing contest have an opportunity to exhibit their best efforts at expository writing or political cartooning in *TIME Lines,* the *TIME* Education Program publication of student writing.

The winner in each of the three categories of the competition receives a $5000 scholarship to the college he or she chooses to attend, a certificate of merit, and a three-year subscription to *TIME.* In addition, up to twenty-five finalists in each category receive a certificate of merit and a one-year subscription to *TIME.*

Forty-seven finalists were selected in the 1983 contest. The May 1983 edition of *TIME Lines* carried these comments about the entries: "We were impressed by the range and depth of the ideas expressed in the hundreds of compositions. . . . You demonstrated that you are interested in and informed on a spectrum of topics ranging from acid rain to poetic forms, from military defense to computer-aided crime, from the philosophy of François Mitterand to the trials of Lech Walesa."

Rules and Procedures

Any student in the ninth through the twelfth grade may participate in the contest. Entries must consist of a 500- to 750-word expository composition in any one of the following categories: the Nation; the World; or Essay. The categories of the contest correspond to the various departments featured weekly in *TIME,* and editors and writers of the magazine participate in the selection of winning entries.

Students must first submit their work to one of their teachers, who then enters the student's composition in the competition. Students should be aware that the contest is not restricted to submissions from English or writing teachers; high school teachers in any subject may enter a student's work. If a participating teacher sponsors a winning entry, a $200 donation will be made to the school's scholarship or activities fund in the name of the teacher. Students interested in entering the contest should be sure to inform their teachers of this added benefit of participation in the contest.

Each entry must be accompanied by the entry blank found in the December or January issue of *Timesavers.* These forms may be obtained by writing directly to the *TIME* Education Program.

Entries are evaluated by a panel of educators and *TIME* staff members. Essay entries are judged on their originality, demonstration of research skills, knowledge of subject matter, and effective use of language, including clarity, spelling, grammar, and punctuation. Time, Inc., reserves the right not to award a prize in any category in which the judges decide there is no meritorious entry. The $5000 scholarship award may be held for two years by the winning student before it is used to pay college costs.

Helpful Hints

The contest literature offers this basic yet important advice to contestants: "Review *TIME* Magazine for a better understanding of the various departments on which the contest is based."

Program Deadlines

Entries must be postmarked no later than March 1. The winners are announced in the May issue of *TIME Lines.*

For Additional Information/Application Forms

Entry blanks can be obtained by writing to:

> TIME Education Program
> Student Writing Contest Entry Department
> P.O. Box 215
> Parsippany, New Jersey 07054

For information about the program, write to the above address or to:

> TIME Education Program
> Time & Life Building
> New York, New York 10020

Union of American Hebrew Congregations—Connie Berlin Memorial Essay Contest

Focus: Writing

Who May Enter: UAHC-affiliated members of Reform Jewish congregations

Entry Requirement: Essay

Awards: (1) $3000 cash award

Deadline: December 1

Sponsor/Administrator: Union of American Hebrew Congregations

The Union of American Hebrew Congregations is the major organization of Reform Jewish congregations in the Western Hemisphere. The UAHC sponsors the annual Connie Berlin Memorial Essay Contest for members of its 750 affiliated temples. A set of Jewish encyclopedias is given to the winner in each of 3 divisions: high school students, college students, and adults. The author of the best essay submitted in all 3 divisions is awarded a cash prize of $3000.

Rules and Procedures

Members of Reform Jewish congregations affiliated with the Union of American Hebrew Congregations are eligible to enter the competition. Participants must submit essays of 2,500–5,000 words (including quoted material and footnotes) on a selected topic. The subject for the 1983–84 contest was "Why I Choose To Be a Jew."

Program Deadlines

The deadline for submitting essays is December 1.

For More Information/Application Forms

Write to: Union of American Hebrew Congregations
836 Fifth Avenue
New York, New York 10021

United States Senate Youth Program

Focus: Leadership

Who May Enter: Students in 11th-12th grades who are elected student government officers; U.S. citizens or permanent residents only. Also open to U.S. students attending DoD schools abroad.

Entry Requirements: Application, exam (for some)

Awards: (104) $2000 scholarships

Deadline: Early autumn

Sponsor/Administrator: William Randolph Hearst Foundation/U.S. Senate Youth Program

---

In 1962 the United States Senate voted unanimously to endorse a nationwide youth program that would bring high school students to Washington, D.C., for an inside view of the workings of the federal government and, in particular, the Senate. The result was the United States Senate Youth Program, funded by the William Randolph Hearst Foundation, which offers both scholarship benefits and a highly educational experience to outstanding high school students.

Two student delegates from each state, the District of Columbia, and U.S. DoD Dependents Schools abroad are chosen to travel to Washington, D.C., for an intensive week of meetings with Senators, Cabinet members, officials of the Departments of Defense and State, and justices of the Supreme Court. The students are greeted by the President and Vice President, and they serve a day of internship in the offices of their respective Senators. In addition, a $2000 scholarship grant is presented to each delegate during the program.

A 1978 survey of the first decade of delegates to the U.S. Senate Youth Program found that a number of former participants were currently holding office or working for the government at the state or federal level. Representative comments from delegates questioned in the survey include the following:

"The Program whetted a growing appetite for public affairs and politics, not only as a result of the tremendous learning experience, but also by exposing me to a fascinating group of intelligent, thoughtful peers who shared my concern for government."

"The Senate Youth Program was my first inside exposure to the public decision-making process. It effectively sensitized me to those experiences and skills that I hope will make possible a long and effective public affairs career."

Rules and Procedures

Any high school junior or senior is eligible to participate provided that he or she has not previously been a delegate to the program, and provided that he or she is currently serving in an elected capacity in any one of the following student government offices:

- student body president, vice president, secretary, or treasurer

- class president, vice president, secretary, or treasurer

- student council representative.

Each student must be a citizen or permanent resident of the United States and be currently enrolled in a public or private secondary school in the state (or the District of Columbia) in which either one of his or her parents or guardians legally resides. Students attending a school located in a state other than the state of legal residence of their parents or guardians are not eligible. The program is also open to students attending Department of Defense Dependents Schools abroad.

The program is administered on the state level by the chief school officer in each state. In most cases, high school officials are asked to select one candidate to be judged in preliminary district competition. The program discourages states from allowing the high schools to choose the student body president as a matter of course; instead, a standardized examination on the American governmental system is distributed to state program administrators for use in selecting delegates, and many states do utilize it.

Participation in the program varies greatly from state to state; in recent years, the number of schools in each state that entered students in the competition has ranged from about 50 to almost 900.

Program Deadlines

Delegates are selected by November 1. The program in Washington, D.C., occurs in late January or early February.

For Additional Information

Information about the program may be obtained by contacting your high school principal or the Chief School Officer in your state (or for students living abroad, the Office of Department of Defense Dependents Schools), or by writing to:

>Program Director
>United States Senate Youth Program
>Suite 502
>690 Market Street
>San Francisco, California 94104

Voice of Democracy Scholarship Program

Focus:	Public speaking
Who May Enter:	Students in 10th-12th grades; U.S. citizens only. Also open to American students abroad.
Entry Requirement:	Short prepared speech. *Advanced level:* tape-recorded speech
Awards:	National: (1) $14,000, (1) $7000, (1) $4500, (1) $3500, (1) $2500, (1) $1000 scholarship State, district, local: cash awards totaling $575,000 (number and amounts vary)
Deadline:	November 30
Sponsor/Administrator:	Veterans of Foreign Wars of the U.S.A. and its Ladies Auxiliary

The Voice of Democracy Scholarship Program, sponsored by the Veterans of Foreign Wars of the U.S.A. and its Ladies Auxiliary, offers high school students an opportunity to win lucrative scholarships and cash benefits. Program competitors must express their views in a 3- to 5-minute script on a selected theme relating to freedom and citizenship. Hundreds of awards that together total more than $600,000 are presented to winners in the VOD Program at the district, state, and national levels.

The top six national winners receive scholarships in amounts ranging from $1000 to the top prize of $14,000. Participation in the national finals is a valuable experience for students in many other ways as well.

Winners from each of the fifty states, the District of Columbia, and American schools overseas are awarded an all-expense-paid, five-day trip to Washington, D.C., where they tour the nation's capital, meet top-ranking government leaders, and gain a better understanding of our American heritage. The national finalists do not take part in a live competition during the Washington program; tape recordings of their scripts are judged for national honors by a panel including members of Congress and top broadcasting executives.

The week-long Washington program culminates in the awards ceremony at the annual Veterans of Foreign Wars Congressional Banquet. The national Voice of Democracy champion delivers his or her speech at this massive gathering, which includes several thousand veterans and "the power and the glory" of Capitol Hill and the Pentagon. For 1983 national winner Melissa Houghton, a junior from Sunbury, Pennsylvania, winning top VOD honors led to an interview on the *Today* show and numerous speaking engagements; these included the chance to deliver her prize-winning script following an address by President Reagan at the VFW convention in New Orleans.

The Voice of Democracy scripts of all fifty-two national finalists are entered in the *Congressional Record,* often along with compliments and honors from their senators and congressional representatives. Even after the VOD program is over, the benefits continue for the national finalists, who are invited to attend the American Academy of Achievement Salute to Excellence weekend (see p. 203), where they have the chance to meet and mingle with national leaders in business, science, sports, and the arts.

Rules and Procedures

The contest is open to all tenth, eleventh, and twelfth grade students, including those attending American schools abroad. U.S. citizenship is required. National winners and first-place state winners are not eligible to participate more than once.

To enter the contest, students in participating high schools prepare and submit a 3- to 5-minute script dealing with the specified VOD theme. Each year a different theme is selected for the contest. Recent themes have included "My Role in Upholding Our Constitution" (1983-84), "Youth—America's Strength" (1982-83), and "Building America Together" (1981-82).

To proceed in the competition, the student submitting the best script in each participating high school must make a professional-quality tape recording of the speech, which then is entered in district competition.

The recordings of winning entrants advance to state-level and finally national-level competition.

Two types of recordings are permitted in the competition: reel-type magnetic tapes at 7½" per second, using single-track equipment, and cassette recordings.

Helpful Hints

Writing the Script—The actual content of the speech is heavily emphasized in the judging. The point values for scoring the recordings follow these guidelines:

Content—35 points
Originality—35 points
Delivery—30 points

Thus, 70 percent of the judging points concern the script itself. In district and state-level contests the judges typically will listen to over twenty-five recordings in succession, all on the same topic. For a script to stand out in such a large pool of contestants, originality and freshness of approach are imperative.

The 35 maximum points for content are assigned based on the script's relation to subject (1–15 points), logical development of ideas (1–10 points), and clarity of ideas (1–10 points).

The 35 points for originality are assigned based on positive approach (1–10 points), imagination (1–10 points), individualistic approach (1–10 points), and human interest appeal (1–5 points).

Delivery—The contest regulations specify that the delivery should be in a natural style. The voices should sound relaxed and conversational rather than oratorical; the script should be spoken, not sung. The 30 points awarded for delivery are assigned for enunciation and pronunciation (10 points), expressiveness (10 points), and sincerity of tone (10 points).

Regarding speed of delivery, contestants should note that the most effective VOD contest recordings are moderately slow and carefully articulated. The delivery should be highly practiced and perfected before the recording is made. Contests are often won on the basis of a single point separating participants—and a single mistake in the delivery could be a contestant's downfall.

Making the Tape—It is strongly suggested that contestants make their recording at a professional studio or radio station, using 7½" magnetic tape rather than cassettes. Before the judging takes place, tapes are carefully inspected for technical quality and the absence of background noise. "Do-it-yourself" jobs will probably lessen your chances of winning a scholarship award.

The approaches taken in the scripts of the fifty-two national finalists in the 1983 Voice of Democracy Program (topic: "Youth—America's Strength") were highly diverse. An examination of excerpts from the winning speeches illustrates several methods, techniques, and literary devices Voice of Democracy contestants may use in their own efforts.

- *Doing the unexpected.* Several of the most effective scripts pointed out the weaknesses commonly associated with youth. Lowell Deo of Texas opened his speech with:

"Young people: those hideous creatures of adolescence—living totally in worn blue denim jeans and buried beneath mound upon mound of greasy, oily hair.

The typical teen is synonymous with poor grades, promiscuity, marijuana, fast cars, and frustrating cases of acne. This is the image of the teen-ager—at least as defined by the television and motion-picture industry—all in the name of humor, but is this image of our youth truly accurate?"

Similarly, Rob Hurst of Louisiana, the fourth-place national winner, wrote, "To be sixteen, a senior in high school, and a future adult is a scary thought, especially when the future of your family, community, and country will rest upon your shoulders. That's why we, the youth, can be America's weakness or strength."

- *Approaching the topic in a novel or uncommon way.* Finding a new interpretation or unexpected meaning in the topic can be a useful device. Michelle Nuszkiewicz of California, fifth-place national winner, wrote:

"On four separate occasions within the last five years, Dewey Hudlow has risked his own life for the sake of saving someone else's.

Bill Kemper has bicycled 919 miles over the Colorado mountain passes in only ten days.

Marila Salsburry began jogging only three years ago and has since competed successfully in world class races.

Now what is it that makes these individuals so extraordinary?

The local lifeguard saves many lives in the course of his job. We are all familiar with teenagers and their ten-speeds and joggers are a common sight on city streets and country roads.

But, Dewey is 51, Bill is 77, and Marila is 73 years of age.

These people acquired the fountain of youth not by counting birthdays but by remaining young at heart. . . .

Youth is actually enthusiasm, endurance, and enjoyment."

- *Use of descriptive language.* Some successful Voice of Democracy contestants scrap the straight expository style and compose highly descriptive, dramatic prose. The results can be very effective, stirring the attention of the listener. Laurence Sumner of Missouri opened his speech with:

"Nothing chills like the cold channel winter wind that comes in over Cambridge in the English mid-country. It blows over a setting that can stun the soul of any American. There, outside the city, lies a monument where the famous 8th Air Force once headquartered. All across a high wall appear the names and states of those American youths who died in the bloody raids over northern Europe. The white crosses that mark the graves of those Americans stand in perfect symmetry and stark testimony to the precious gift of the youth of America that was then laid at the altar of freedom."

Rhode Island winner Marywanda Fandino began her script on a striking key:

"Scene I:
 It is black—deep and dark. Its shape is irregular. On it are engraved the names of 57,939 young Americans. It is made of granite—strong, resilient, reflective. Standing before it one can see a reflection peering among the crowded names, as though someone were looking out from within the monument. One can easily imagine them as they were—a confident stance, minds alert and aware, graceful gestures, darting eyes—the embodiment of youth. They laughed, lived, cried, they thought, dreamed, stood and died.
"Scene II:
 Atop a hill, four young men strive against the wind and against the odds to raise a piece of cloth bearing several stripes and a multitude of stars. This monument symbolizes the relationship between the United States and its youth."

These excerpts offer just a small sampling of the approaches taken by the 1982–83 national finalists. As one might expect, the speeches abounded with quotes from philosophers, poets, and world leaders. The winners ran the gamut in their styles and techniques, but all used creative methods to make their messages interesting and important.

Program Deadlines

School and district-level Voice of Democracy contests are scheduled in the fall and are completed by the end of November. State winners are selected in January, and the national finals are held in early March.

For Additional Information

Contact the principal or teacher in your school who supervises the program or a local Veterans of Foreign Wars Post, or write to:

Voice of Democracy Program
VFW National Headquarters
Broadway at 34th Street
Kansas City, Missouri 64111

Washington Crossing Foundation Scholarship Awards

Focus: Leadership

Who May Enter: Students in 12th grade planning a career in government service; U.S. citizens only

Entry Requirements: Application, essay, recommendation. *Advanced level:* interviews

Awards: (2) $2500 scholarships (1 to a resident or student in 1 of the 13 original colonies); additional scholarships (number and amounts vary)

Deadline: March 1

Sponsor/Administrator: Washington Crossing Foundation

The Washington Crossing Foundation sponsors an annual scholarship program for high school seniors planning a career in politics or government service. The aim of the program reflects the stated conviction of the Foundation, that "if our country is to continue to progress, we must have thoroughly trained, dedicated young people to carry on our government's work in future years."

Two students are awarded scholarships of $2500 each. Winners receive $1000 in the first year; an additional $500 is renewable annually for three subsequent years over the course of four years of study at the college or university of the scholarship recipient's choice. One of the two scholarships is given to a student who lives or attends a school in one of the thirteen original colonies. Additional scholarships for program finalists receiving honorable mention vary from year to year depending on available funding; four 1-year awards were granted in 1982.

Rules and Procedures

The competition is open to all high school seniors planning to pursue a career in local, state, or federal government service in the United States. Participants must be U.S. citizens.

Each applicant must write an essay of not more than 200 words stating why he or she plans a career in government service. Scholarship candidates must also submit a letter of recommendation from their high school principal or guidance counselor, evaluating the student's accomplishments, both academic and nonacademic, and describing in particular any preparation relevant to the career choice. Candidates may, if they wish, submit other documentation (such as additional recommendations, class rank, and GPA) in support of their application.

Applicants are ranked on the basis of their essay, recommendations, and other documentation. The top five percent in the rankings are selected as semifinalists. Semifinalists are interviewed by phone concerning specific aspects of their applications and their views on current events. A small group of finalists is chosen, and these students are then given a second telephone interview. The two top winners are selected from among these finalists, as are several additional recipients of honorable mention scholarships, when the necessary funding is available.

Helpful Hints

The panel of judges is composed of at least three members of the Board of Trustees of the Washington Crossing Foundation, one member of the Washington Crossing Park Commission, and a prominent educator. The contest literature states that the judges base their decision on the applicant's purpose in choosing a career in government; on his or her understanding of the requirements and preparation needed for such a career; on qualities of sincerity and leadership that the applicant exhibits; and on his or her historical perspective.

In preparing the essay, students must strive above all to be concise and direct. Because the length of the essay is restricted to 200 words or less, scholarship candidates must attempt to articulate their views clearly yet economically. By carefully confining the essay to one's "viewpoint, attitude, and purpose" in choosing a career, as the rules specify, this can be accomplished. The essay should not include descriptions of the last student council meeting at which the applicant spoke; the judges are looking for a student's sense of purpose and career direction.

The true test of scholarship candidates comes at the semifinalist stage of competition. The phone interviews for both semifinalists and finalists can be very lengthy and demanding. Contestants should be ready to answer questions about the material they submitted in their applications. The major portion of the interview will center on the student's views on current events, however. Students will be asked to explain and defend their views on topics such as foreign affairs, defense, economics, politics, and social issues. They should be prepared to answer probing questions on these subjects.

Holly Yeager of Pennsylvania, a scholarship winner in the 1982 competition, wrote in her application of her plans to join the Foreign Service and her interest in world events. She advises: "Be prepared for anything—I was interviewed in French over the phone as part of the program! Also, demonstrate a thorough understanding of current events, and be able to clearly state and back up your opinions."

Program Deadlines

Applications must be submitted by March 1. Semifinalists are announced in mid-March. Scholarship winners receive their awards at a ceremony in Pennsylvania's Washington Crossing Historic Park in April.

For More Information

See your high school principal or guidance counselor, or write to:

> Washington Crossing Foundation
> P.O. Box 1976
> Washington Crossing, Pennsylvania 18977

Westinghouse Science Talent Search

Focus:	Science, math, computers, engineering
Who May Enter:	Students in 12th grade. Also open to students in PR and DoD schools abroad.
Entry Requirements:	Application, independent research project. *Advanced level:* Project exhibit at Science Talent Institute, Washington, D.C.
Awards:	(1) $12,000, (2) $10,000, (3) $7500, (4) $5000, (30) $500 scholarships
Deadline:	December 15
Sponsor/Administrator:	Westinghouse Electric Corp., Westinghouse Educational Foundation/Science Service

The Westinghouse Science Talent Search is widely recognized as one of the most prestigious scholarship competitions for high school students interested in the sciences. Now in its fifth decade, the program is sponsored jointly by Westinghouse Electric Corporation and the Westinghouse Educational Foundation and is administered by Science Service, a nonprofit organization that promotes the public understanding of science. The competition centers on students' independent research projects in mathematical or scientific fields, including the behavioral and social sciences. Placing among the contest's 300 Honors Group students puts one in an elite circle of the nation's most talented and promising young science scholars. From this group, 40 top winners are chosen to attend the national Science Talent Institute in Washington, D.C., a 5-day program during which students attend special events, meet prominent scientists, and have the opportunity to share interests and build friendships with fellow winners. During this program, the national finalists are judged at challenging interview sessions that are used to select the 10 winners of the sizable 4-year Westinghouse Science Scholarships, which range from $5000 to the top prize of $12,000. Scholarships of $500 are awarded to the remaining 30 finalists chosen to attend the Science Talent Institute.

Science Service remarks in its literature, "To be named a winner or member of the Honors Group in the Science Talent Search is one of the highest recommendations for admission to leading educational institutions." This claim is not exaggerated; numerous winners have been accepted at top-notch colleges and universities, including MIT, Princeton, and Harvard.

Furthermore, "top 40" Westinghouse winners often don't have to wait long to start taking advantage of their recognition professionally. Recent winners report that their Science Talent Search awards have been instrumental in helping them gain summer employment and other opportunities in the scientific community.

All national winners receive recommendations from Science Service to the college of their choice, but the prestige of the competition extends beyond the upper echelon of winners to embrace the Honors Group and state-level winners as well. Honors Group students are recommended to all U.S. colleges as worthy of admission and scholarship aid if needed. Winners in the State Science Talent Searches (currently held in 36 states and the District of Columbia) also receive college recommendations and are eligible for financial assistance.

Beyond recognition and scholarship grants, many national finalists stress the sense of accomplishment and the chance to interact with other students and with scientific leaders as valuable aspects of the contest. "I don't think people entering the contest should make the scholarship money their main goal," remarks Ling Ping Chen, a student at the Bronx High School of Science and one of the top 40 winners in 1983. "I think they should enter it for the honor of being recognized as students who have gone beyond expectations of regular school work and have had the drive to work by themselves on topics they're interested in. They should not think of it as a contest but rather as an unforgettable experience and a time to learn from each other and meet other people in a field they're interested in."

A number of leading Westinghouse participants receive sponsorship each year from various private sources to attend the American Academy of Achievement Salute to Excellence weekend (see p. 203), where the first-place winner receives the national champion "Golden Eagle" honors. Also held in Washington, D.C., the Academy weekend presents a chance for Westinghouse contest winners to be reunited and also gives them an opportunity to talk with numerous Nobel Prize winners and innovators in medicine, science, and technology.

Rules and Procedures

High school seniors only are eligible to take part in the Westinghouse Science Talent Search program. Teachers or other school officials must place requests to Science Service to obtain entry materials for any of their students who wish to participate.

To enter the competition, the student must submit a report roughly 1,000 words long on an independent research project in the physical sciences, behavioral or social sciences, engineering, mathematics, or biological sciences (excluding live vertebrate experimentation). The research project must be the work of a single individual and must extend beyond regular high school course work; group projects are not eligible.

No projects involving live vertebrate animal experimentation are eligible, except for projects involving behavioral observations of animals in their natural habitat. There are extensive federal regulations for the protection of human subjects in behavioral and biomedical research; applicants should read carefully these regulations, which can be found in the booklet distributed by Science Service providing detailed instructions on how to write up the report for the program.

Each entry must include a Personal Data Blank filled out by the student and his or her teachers and principal, which details the student's academic accomplishments as well as any other information that demonstrates his or her promise as a creative scientist. Students must also prepare answers to such questions as "Describe your creativity" and "What do you plan to be doing ten years from now?" on the Personal Data Blank. In addition, a secondary school record must accompany the entry, to include available national test scores (e.g., PSAT/NMSQT, SAT/ACT, and National Education Development Tests).

The research project reports are each evaluated by two or more Science Service judges, who are assisted by a panel of independent scientists and engineers. The selection of the Honors Group and the national winners is based on an evaluation of all available data, but the greatest weight in the judging is placed on the project report.

Each of the 40 finalists invited to attend the national competition in Washington, D.C., must bring to the Science Talent Institute a project exhibit suitable for public display. The exhibit will have no bearing on the judging for scholarships, and it need not be based on the project report submitted in the competition.

Recipients of Westinghouse scholarship grants must apply their scholarships toward a course of study in science or engineering at a degree-granting institution of higher education in the United States that has been approved by the Science Service scholarship committee.

Helpful Hints

Now a student at the Massachusetts Institute of Technology, 1983 national champion Paul Ning began work on his research project during his junior year at the Bronx High School of Science. He states, "I proposed several problems in number theory and proceeded to solve them, some of them completely and others incompletely. This began with experimental calculations, then conjectures, and finally proofs of the valid results."

He advises Science Talent Search contestants that "the project should definitely contain original research. If you are not completely familiar with the field about which you are writing, you will have to become so in order to write authoritatively. This can come about through summer programs or independent research and reading." Paul spent two summers attending math programs at college campuses, and he observes, "Although I did these primarily out of my own interest in learning the subject, I found that they were excellent training for the completion of my project."

Paul Ning's experience and that of many other national finalists serve to confirm the following advice offered to aspiring Science Talent Search competitors:

- Do your independent research project in a field you are genuinely interested in.

- It is a good idea to start early on the research project rather than waiting for the senior year to begin preparation.

- Attending special math or science programs at colleges or universities for one or more summers can be very useful, both as a means of conducting research and to improve one's knowledge of the scientific field.

Although the contest is open to students with projects in the social sciences (anthropology, economics, political science, sociology, and so on), recent Westinghouse finalists cannot recall any national winner submitting a project in one of these areas. Winning projects usually concern the physical or life sciences, mathematics, engineering, computers, or other "hard-core" scientific fields. However, this is not to imply that social science projects cannot be successful entries. Entrants should note that a social science–related project is more likely to receive favorable consideration if it employs an empirical approach and the kind of scientific reasoning typical of math or physical science experimentation.

Program Deadlines

Entries must be received at Science Service no later than December 15. The five-day National Science Talent Institute program in Washington, D.C., is held in early March.

For Additional Information/Application Forms

Write to: Science Service
1719 N Street, N.W.
Washington, D.C. 20036

Young Playwrights Festival

Focus: Writing

Who May Enter: Anyone under 19 yrs of age (as of 7/1)

Entry Requirement: Play script

Awards: Royalties from professional productions; scholarship awards from other sponsors (number and amounts vary)

Deadline: July 1

Sponsor/Administrator: Foundation of the Dramatists Guild

The annual Young Playwrights Festival is the only national competition for teenage playwrights. Sponsored by the Foundation of the Dramatists Guild, it offers that rare opportunity by which an unknown yet talented teenage author can be catapulted overnight into the limelight of the theatrical world. Each year the scripts of a handful of authors, aged 18 or younger, are chosen for full-scale, staged productions by the New York Shakespeare Festival, a leading Off-Broadway theater company. (In 1983, four such scripts were chosen.) The winning authors are given the opportunity to attend and contribute to rehearsal sessions, and they receive royalties on revenues generated by their play's performance. Past productions of Young Playwrights Festival plays have included well-known actors and some of Broadway's leading directors, such as Michael Bennett (Tony Award winner for *A Chorus Line* and *Dreamgirls*).

In addition to the Off-Broadway productions of top entries in the festival, a number of other plays receive professionally staged readings before an invited audience. In the process, the authors who reach this semifinalist level of competition are also given the chance to work closely with leading professional playwrights.

The scripts of winning plays from the Young Playwrights Festival are published by Avon Books as part of the Bard Series. Past contest winners at all levels have succeeded in launching careers in television, regional theatre, and Off-Off-Broadway. An added bonus of the program: each year New York University makes available a $2500 tuition scholarship to one of the festival finalists.

While the opportunities and thrills the competition offers to the group of top winners are impressive, all entrants benefit from participation in the festival. The panel selecting the winning plays, which has included such theatrical luminaries as Jules Feiffer and Stephen Sondheim, sends all participants detailed, written evaluations of their entries.

Jules Feiffer, who is president of the Foundation of the Dramatists Guild, remarked on the first annual festival in 1982: "The surprise of our first year was in the depth and quality of the entries. The good news is that talented young playwrights are letting us hear their voices, ideas, humor, and anger for the first time—and it is as clear and welcome a sound as any heard today."

Stephen Gutwillig, a winning playwright in the 1982 festival, commented on being selected: "I've learned a great deal so far and I intend to keep right on learning. The Young Playwrights Festival has been one of the greatest things ever to happen to me, and I'm more thrilled than I could possibly express at the thought of real actors speaking my words."

Rules and Procedures

Authors submitting scripts must be under the age of 19 as of the program deadline (July 1). There are no restrictions as to the play's subject matter, style, form, or length. Collaborations and group-written plays are eligible so long as all contributors meet the age requirements.

Plays submitted to previous Young Playwrights Festivals cannot be reentered in subsequent competitions. Film scripts and screenplays are not eligible, nor are adaptations of other authors' work.

Authors should include with their submission a brief cover letter about themselves and how they became interested in writing their play. Festival participants may have to submit proof of their age.

Helpful Hints

The Foundation of the Dramatists Guild offers this advice to young authors who plan to enter scripts in the competition:

- "In plays, the story is told through speech and action rather than simple description. Avoid using a narrator if possible.

- "Stage directions are useful, but don't overdo them.

- "Avoid too many characters—we suggest that you try to limit the number of actors required to no more than about nine or ten. This will facilitate casting.

- "In the theatre, unlike film or television, you cannot switch easily from one elaborate setting to another. Keep in mind that whatever you write has to be acted on a stage in front of an audience.

- "Have a look at a printed play script to see the way you put things on a page."

Gerald Chapmen, artistic director of the Young Playwrights Festival, has observed, "What we're looking for is work that shows originality and freshness and isn't just a TV ripoff. The best plays we get from young people deal with the world around them. My advice to any young person writing a play is to write about what you know—then it will be authentic and genuine." (*The Star Ledger*, Newark, NJ, May 29, 1983)

The Foundation of the Dramatists Guild conducts 80 workshops for young playwrights in grades 4 through 12 who live in the New York City area. Two of the winners in the 1983 festival had attended such workshops before entering the contest. For potential young authors in New York City who are interested in the Young Playwrights Festival, the workshop program is a valuable tool to gain experience and skill in writing plays.

Descriptions of Some Winning Entries

The following is a list of winning authors in the 1982 festival, accompanied by brief descriptions of their plays (prepared by the Foundation of the Dramatists Guild).

ADAM BERGER, aged 8, from New York City. "It's Time for a Change" tells the story of Kirk, who is not good at school sports. One day he springs a surprise on his classmates.

JULIET GARSON, 13, from New York City. "Nowhere" is about two friends who hatch a startling plot to make the city parks safe for girls to play in.

STEPHEN GUTWILLIG, 17, from New York City. "In the Way" focuses on the relationship between father and son on the day of the mother's funeral.

JENNIE LITT, 17, from University Heights, Ohio. "Epiphany" is set in an exclusive English private school where the arrival of a new boy and his sister upsets a love affair between two of the boys.

KENNETH LONERGAN, 18, from New York City. "The Rennings Children" are Paul, a mental patient, and his sister, Mary, who unsuccessfully tries to get him out of the hospital.

SHOSHANA MARCHAND, 17, from San Francisco. "Half Fare" is about the conflict of values between an adolescent girl and her 37-year-old hippie father.

JOHN McNAMARA, 18, from Grand Rapids, Michigan. "Present Tense" is a comedy about the illusions and anxieties of a teenager in love who thinks he is too ordinary to be loved in return.

PETER MURPHY, 17, from West Hartford, Connecticut. "Bluffing" is a lively game which six men play behind each other's backs around a poker table.

LYNETTE M. SERRANO, 17, from New York City. "The Bronx Zoo" is about a Puerto Rican family living in the South Bronx and striving in their different ways to survive the violence of a tough neighborhood.

ANNE P. WIESE, 17, from New York City. "Coleman, S.D." is the place where two girls and a boy meet every summer and share each other's dreams, until one year their friendship irreparably breaks.

Program Deadlines

The deadline for submitting scripts is July 1.

For Additional Information

Write to: Young Playwrights Festival
The Foundation of the Dramatists Guild
234 West 44th Street
New York, NY 10036

APPENDIX: THE REWARDS OF WINNING

The following two programs describe "super awards" that come with success in previous academic achievement or competitive performance. Students cannot apply to these programs directly. They can, however, maximize their chances to be chosen by entering various contests mentioned in this book. To participate in the American Academy of Achievement, for example, one must be a high-level winner in certain other contests that are named in the description of the AAA.

To be considered for the Presidential Scholars Program, students must have taken the SAT or ACT and have released information that they provided to the Student Search Service (ETS) or the Student Profile Section (ACT), or have entered one of the ARTS competitions described on pages 46 through 48.

American Academy of Achievement—Salute to Excellence Program

Each year, more than 300 outstanding high school students spend an all-expense-paid weekend exchanging ideas with America's greatest achievers—including Nobel laureates and winners of Pulitzer Prizes, Academy Awards, and Super Bowl competitions; leading government policymakers and top brass at the Pentagon, CIA, and FBI; and chief executive officers of *Fortune* 500 companies. This unique event—the Salute to Excellence—is sponsored by the American Academy of Achievement. The brainchild of Brian Reynolds, a former photographer for *Life* magazine, the program brings the great achievers of today together with the great achievers of tomorrow for a stimulating and inspirational experience.

Students invited to participate in the program receive either of the Academy's two prestigious awards—the Golden Eagle or the Golden Scroll.

The Golden Eagle—a gold-trimmed commemorative plate—is awarded to champions of America's top youth competitions. In 1983, Golden Eagle recipients included national winners in the Elks Most Valuable Student competition, the Veterans of Foreign Wars Voice of Democracy contest, the Westinghouse Science Talent Search, the International Science and Engineering Fair, the America's Junior Miss Program, the Future Business Leaders of America competition, and Junior Achievement. Top high school athletes in football, basketball, hockey, swimming, and golf were also honored. In addition, a group of "whiz kids"—teenagers with IQs of 180–200 who were enrolled in special programs at Johns Hopkins University and the University of Washington—received the Golden Eagle distinction.

Numerous state and local representatives to the Salute to Excellence program receive the framed certificate known as the Golden Scroll. The selections are based on recommendations from the Academy's National Advisory Council, which includes directors of numerous organizations and scholarship programs included in this book. In 1983, recipients of the award included all state winners in the VFW Voice of Democracy contest as well as numerous winners in the Westinghouse Science Talent Search, Presidential Scholars Program, National Merit Scholarship Program, National Achievement Scholarship Program, and other competitions. High school valedictorians, salutatorians, student body presidents, and school newspaper editors are among other students awarded the Golden Scroll for their outstanding achievement. The Academy also invites honor students from across the nation to attend this annual event.

Although the primary purpose of the American Academy of Achievement is to inspire youths "to raise their sights high, to excel in their endeavors," the Academy also honors fifty great men and women with the Golden Plate award as part of the Salute to Excellence program. The weekend activities revolve around short seminars presented by these adult recipients of the Golden Plate award. In addressing the students, the "Captains of Achievement" talk about their struggles to achieve success. They also discuss their current work and future plans, and they offer advice to young people on their career aspirations. A lively question-and-answer session follows each speech.

As an added benefit of the program, students have numerous opportunities throughout the weekend to talk informally with the Captains of Achievement. Because open seating exists at all meals, a student walking into the dining room and spotting a personal hero can join the great achiever for food and conversation. In addition, students can meet and mingle with the distinguished adult participants in the program during leisure time spent in the hotel reception rooms, on the tennis court, and even at the late-night dances held for students and "courageous adults." Many of the Academy's student winners have remarked on how personable and accessible the adult achievers have been in the congenial atmosphere of the weekend gathering.

United States Presidential Scholars Program

Perhaps the highest honor a high school student in the United States can attain is to be named a Presidential Scholar. In addition to being recognized as belonging to a small group of America's most promising students, the Presidential Scholars participate in the Presidential Scholars National Recognition Week, a program of special events in Washington, D.C., culminating in a ceremony at the White House.

The Commission on Presidential Scholars, a group of private citizens appointed by the President to select the Presidential Scholars, notes the following in its 1984 fact sheet:

The Presidential Scholars Program was established more than twenty years ago to recognize and honor our nation's most distinguished high school seniors. The Program was extended in 1979 to include recognition of students with exceptional talent in the visual, creative, and performing arts. One hundred forty-one students are chosen annually from among the most outstanding graduating seniors in the United States. Those students who become Presidential Scholars are chosen on the basis of their accomplishments in many areas—academic success, artistic talent, leadership, and involvement in school and community. The Scholars are representative of the promise for greatness in young people. In honoring the Presidential Scholars, the President symbolically honors all American youth of high potential.

Since the program's inception, more than 2,500 distinguished young people have been honored as Presidential Scholars. The majority of students are chosen on the basis of broad academic achievement. Students may not apply individually to the academic component of the program, nor may their schools nominate them. All high school seniors are automatically identified for the program if they have scored well on either the College Board's Scholastic Aptitude Test (SAT) or the Assessment of the American College Testing Program (ACT) and have authorized release of information through the College Board's Student Search Service or the ACT's Student Profile Section. After a review of the student profiles and descriptive questionnaires, some 1,500 students are identified as potential candidates. These students are asked to affirm their candidacy and to submit such materials as essays, self-assessments, and secondary school transcripts in support of their candidacy.

From a pool of 500 students who are chosen as finalists, the Commission on Presidential Scholars selects one young man and one young woman from each state, the District of Columbia, and Puerto Rico. Two students are chosen from families of U.S. citizens living abroad, and 15 students are chosen at large. In addition, 20 students are chosen for recognition on the basis of their achievement in the visual or performing arts or in creative writing. This group is selected from among students who participate in the Arts Recognition and Talent Search Program (see page 42).

Those students chosen by the Commission are awarded the Presidential Scholar medallion, which commemorates their designation as Scholars by the President of the United States. There is no provision for a monetary award within the executive order establishing the program. However, cash grants, referred to as educational stipends, have been given in past years, and such awards may continue to be made available from private sources.

For National Recognition Week, the Presidential Scholars are invited to Washington, D.C., as guests of the Commission, where they are honored by their elected representatives and by other public officials. During their weeklong visit to Washington, the Scholars meet with senators, congressional representatives, and Supreme Court justices as well as educators, musicians, scientists, and distinguished individuals in other fields. They visit the memorials and museums of the nation's capital and attend receptions held in their honor. The program culminates in the presentation of the medallions, and parents are invited to accompany their sons and daughters to the White House ceremony.

INTEREST AREA INDEX

The Arts
Arts Recognition and Talent Search
    Dance
    Music
    Theater
    Visual Arts
    Writing
Broadcast Music Inc. Awards to Student Composers
International Piano Recording Competition
Scholastic Awards Program
    Art
    Photography
    Writing

Business and Vocational Skills
Aid Association for Lutherans Competitive Nursing Scholarship Program
Aid Association for Lutherans Vocational-Technical School Scholarship
    Program
Best Products Foundation Scholarship Program
Future Business Leaders of America–Phi Beta Lambda—Mr. and Ms. Future
    Business Leader Awards
Graphic Arts Technical Foundation Scholarship Program
James F. Lincoln Arc Welding Awards Program
Junior Achievement Awards Program
National 4-H Awards Programs
National Society, Daughters of the American Revolution—Caroline E. Holt
    Educational Fund
TIME Education Program Student Writing Contest

General
Aid Association for Lutherans All-College Scholarship Program
American Association for Gifted Children—Mary Jane and Jerome A. Straka
    Scholarship Fund

American Mensa Education and Research Foundation Scholarship Program
America's Junior Miss Program
Educational Communications Scholarship Program
Elks National Foundation Most Valuable Student Scholarship Contest
Jostens Foundation National Scholarship Program
NAACP Roy Wilkins Scholarship
National Achievement Program for Outstanding Negro Students
National Honor Society Scholarship Awards Program
National Merit Scholarship Program

Humanities and Foreign Languages

American Association of Teachers of German Awards Program
American Association of Teachers of Italian National Contest
American Classical League/National Junior Classical League—National Latin
   Exam
National History Day
National Society, Daughters of the American Revolution—American History
   Scholarship Award

Leadership, Citizenship, and Community Service

Century III Leaders Program
J. Edgar Hoover Foundation Scholarships
Jostens Foundation National Scholarship Program
National 4-H Awards Programs
Soroptimist Foundation Youth Citizenship Awards
United States Senate Youth Program
Washington Crossing Foundation Scholarship Awards

Public Speaking

American Legion National High School Oratorical Contest
National 4-H Awards Programs
National Future Farmers of America Public Speaking Contests
National Society, Sons of the American Revolution—Douglass G. High
   Historical Oration Contest
Optimist International Oratorical Contest
Voice of Democracy Scholarship Program

Science, Math, Computers, Engineering

American Association for Gifted Children—Mary Jane and Jerome A. Straka
   Scholarship Fund
Associated General Contractors Education and Research Foundation—
   Undergraduate Scholarship Program
Bell Laboratories Engineering Scholarship Program
International Science and Engineering Fair
National Science Teachers Association/*Discover* Magazine Science Scholarship
   Program
National Society of Professional Engineers—Engineering Scholarships
Society of Women Engineers Scholarship Program
TIME Education Program Student Writing Contest
Westinghouse Science Talent Search

Writing and Journalism
Arts Recognition and Talent Search
Century III Leaders Program
Guideposts Youth Writing Contest
National Federation of Press Women—High School Journalism Contest
National History Day
National Science Teachers Association/*Discover* Magazine Science Scholarship
    Program
President's Committee on Employment of the Handicapped—National
    Journalism Contest
Quill and Scroll Society—Edward J. Nell Memorial Scholarships
Scholastic Writing Awards
Scripps-Howard Foundation Scholarships
That's Incredible Scholarship Award
TIME Education Program Student Writing Contest
Union of American Hebrew Congregations—Connie Berlin Memorial Essay
    Contest
Young Playwrights Festival

Have You Seen These Other Publications from Peterson's Guides?

The College Money Handbook 1985:
The Complete Guide to Expenses,
Scholarships, Loans, Jobs, and Special Aid
Programs at Four-Year Colleges
SECOND EDITION
Editor: Karen C. Hegener

The only book that describes the complete picture of costs and financial aid at accredited four-year colleges in the United States. The book is divided into three sections: an overview of the financial aid process and ways to make it work for you; cost and aid profiles of each college, showing need-based and merit scholarship programs available; and directories listing colleges by the type of financial aid programs they offer. October 1984.

8½" x 11", 500 pages (approx.)   Stock no. 2820
ISBN 0-87866-282-0   **$12.95** paperback

Your Own Financial Aid Factory:
The Guide to Locating College Money
FIFTH EDITION
Robert Leider

This completely updated edition provides a step-by-step explanation of the financial aid process, describes over 90,000 scholarships at more than 1,000 colleges, and details cooperative education programs, grants, and loans available from the federal government. October 1984.

6" x 9", 190 pages (approx.)   Stock no. 2952
ISBN 0-87866-295-2   **$7.95** paperback

Peterson's Annual Guides/Undergraduate Study
Guide to Four-Year Colleges 1985
FIFTEENTH EDITION
Managing Editor: Kim R. Kaye
Book Editor: Joan H. Hunter

The largest, most up-to-date guide to all 1,900 accredited four-year colleges in the United States and Canada. Contains concise college profiles, a reader guidance section, and two-page "Messages from the Colleges" that are found in no other guide. September 1984.

8½" x 11", 2,100 pages (approx.)
                              Stock no. 2316
ISBN 0-87866-231-6   **$12.95** paperback

Peterson's Annual Guides/Undergraduate Study
Guide to Two-Year Colleges 1985
FIFTEENTH EDITION
Managing Editor: Kim R. Kaye
Book Editor: Joan H. Hunter

This Guide covers over 1,450 accredited U.S. institutions that grant associate degrees. It contains basic college profiles, 1,800-word college essays written by admissions directors who chose to provide in-depth information, and directories of colleges by geographical area and by major. It serves as a companion volume to the *Guide to Four-Year Colleges 1985.* October 1984.

8½" x 11", 400 pages (approx.)   Stock no. 2324
ISBN 0-87866-232-4   **$9.95** paperback

SAT Success:
Peterson's Study Guide to English and Math
Skills for College Entrance Examinations:
SAT, ACT, and PSAT
Joan Davenport Carris and Michael R. Crystal

This brand-new step-by-step text is designed as an effective self-instruction aid to build both the skills and the confidence of students preparing for college entrance examinations. Quiz-filled verbal and math sections plus mock SATs and actual questions from recent tests are included for practice.

8½" x 11", 380 pages   Stock no. 2081
ISBN 0-87866-208-1   **$8.95** paperback

Peterson's Competitive Colleges
THIRD EDITION
Editor: Karen C. Hegener

The only book that determines college selectivity from objective data—and gives you the facts to work with. *Peterson's Competitive Colleges* presents a full page of comparative data for each of 302 colleges that consistently have more undergraduate applicants—with above-average abilities—than they can accept.

7" x 10", 291 pages   Stock no. 2677
ISBN 0-87866-267-7   **$7.95** paperback

Peterson's Guide to College Admissions:
Getting into the College of Your Choice
THIRD EDITION
R. Fred Zuker and Karen C. Hegener

This updated edition takes students behind the scenes at college admissions offices and gives current advice from admissions directors all across the country. Contains dozens of campus photos and capsule profiles of 1,700 four-year colleges.

8½" x 11", 366 pages   Stock no. 2243
ISBN 0-87866-224-3   **$9.95** paperback

The Athlete's Game Plan
for College and Career
Stephen Figler and Howard Figler

The first book to deal with *all* the commitments of a student athlete—academic achievement, athletic responsibilities, and career selection—and to show how to keep them in balance. Covers college selection, dealing with recruiters, financial aid, eligibility for college sports, study skills, coping strategies, education and athletics as bridges to career success, and job-hunting techniques. June 1984.

6" x 9", 250 pages (approx.)   Stock no. 2669
ISBN 0-87866-266-9   **$9.95** paperback

College 101
Dr. Ronald T. Farrar

The first book to answer the questions college-bound students most often ask— about money, health, social life, sex, and academic concerns. Written with empathy, common sense, and knowledge, this book can serve as a springboard to frank discussions of all college-related topics. July 1984.

6" x 9", 125 pages (approx.)   Stock no. 2693
ISBN 0-87866-269-3   **$6.95** paperback

How to Order

These publications are available from all good booksellers, or you may order direct from **Peterson's Guides, Dept. 4610, P.O. Box 2123, Princeton, New Jersey 08540.** Please note that prices are necessarily subject to change without notice.

- Enclose full payment for each book, plus postage and handling charges as follows:

Amount of Order	4th-Class Postage and Handling Charges
$1-$10	$1.25
$10.01-$20	$2.00
$20.01-$40	$3.00
$40.01 +	Add $1.00 shipping and handling for every additional $20 worth of books ordered.

Place your order TOLL-FREE by calling 800-225-0261 between 8:30 A.M. and 4:30 P.M.

Eastern time, Monday through Friday. Telephone orders over $15 may be charged to your charge card; institutional and trade orders over $20 may be billed. From New Jersey, Alaska, Hawaii, and outside the United States, call 609-924-5338.

- For faster shipment via United Parcel Service (UPS), add $2.00 over and above the appropriate fourth-class book-rate charges listed.
- Bookstores and tax-exempt organizations should contact us for appropriate discounts.
- You may charge your order to VISA, MasterCard, or American Express. Minimum charge order: $15. Please include the name, account number, and validation and expiration dates for charge orders.
- New Jersey residents should add 6% sales tax to the cost of the books, excluding the postage and handling charge.
- Write for a free catalog describing all of our latest publications.